Designing for Heritage

Designing for Heritage: Contemporary Visitor Centres

Ruth Dalton

First published in 2017 by Lund Humphries
Office 3, Book House
261A City Road
London
EC1V 1JX
UK

www.lundhumphries.com

ISBN 978-1-84822-214-4

A Cataloguing-in-Publication record for this
book is available from the British Library.

All images by the Author unless otherwise
stated.

Cover: The Giant's Causeway visitor centre at
dusk, Heneghan Peng Architects, photograph
by Hufton & Crow

Frontispiece: Semi-enclosed spatial relationship
between the Cutty Sark and its visitor centre

Designed by Mark Thomson
Printed in Slovenia

To Aidan and Amelia, for keeping me company
on so many of my trips to see the visitor centres
and for your patience when I then spent hours
taking photographs.

Contents

Preface and Acknowledgements

The initial seed, from which this book germinated, came from the Masters in Architecture students at the University of Northumbria. For a few years now, we have been running a 'live projects' studio in the first year of the MArch programme. In this studio, we work with real clients on real projects and, as such, there is always a chance that one of the students' schemes might result in being built. In recent years, two of the most memorable (and successful) projects have been The Land of Oak & Iron Heritage Centre, which is to be built at Winlaton Mill, and forthcoming Angel of the North Visitor Centre. The student who created the successful design, from which The Land of Oak & Iron Heritage Centre has been developed, was Matt Glover and this scheme has now succeeded in attracting Heritage Lottery Funding with the client hoping to start building work in 2017 to open in time for the Great Exhibition of the North in summer 2018. The Angel of the North Visitor Centre has been submitted for pre-application planning permission with a view to submitting it for full planning application by the end of 2017.

During our weekly studio tutorials, students would frequently show me precedent studies of award-winning visitor centres from all around the country, often built by high profile architectural practices and often having won prestigious architectural awards. However, it was clear, that despite such a wealth of material and precedent case studies there was no single source-book for the students (or practitioners) to use and it struck me that this was

a book that was surely waiting to happen (if only someone would get around to writing it).

If this was the 'seed' for the book, then the 'water' came from Valerie Rose from Lund Humphries Publishers, towards the end of 2015. Valerie had been the editor for my book on the Seattle Central Library (Hölscher and Dalton, 2016),[1] and contacted me to ask whether I was interested in writing a book for a wider professional audience. Naturally, like any academic, I had a 'bucket list' of future books, which I sent to Valerie. I just happened to mention, almost in passing, my observation that there was a need for a book on the architecture of visitor centres. It was this proposal that struck a chord with Valerie as, by coincidence, this was one of the topics which she had already flagged up as being a particularly interesting one and about which there had been surprisingly little written. The most bizarre moment, for me, came when I read the description that Valerie had already written about 'a book on visitor centres' and initially thought that I was re-reading my own description (so close were our two visions of what this book should be).

For me, what was (and still is) particularly interesting about visitor centres was that they are, almost by definition, sited in some of the most sensitive landscapes in the country and therefore issues of 'place' and 'context' are paramount to their design. And, of all building types, they are the one that most exemplifies a need to design for the one-off, first-time and unfamiliar visitor; they can be seen as being the ultimate visitor-focused or user-centric building, which was something that I, along with my long-standing research collaborator, Christoph Hölscher, had already been researching for more than a decade. And so, by the end of January 2016, the decision had been made to write this book.

At the same time, I had the opportunity to apply for a sabbatical from Northumbria University, which I was subsequently awarded. And so, this book feels as if it has been the result of many serendipitous (and fortunate) events that simply happened to coincide. Indeed, in retrospect, this book could not have been completed without the sabbatical awarded to me by Northumbria University (as well as their financial support permitting me to travel to all of the visitor centres mentioned in this book). This was my first sabbatical, despite having been an academic since 2000, and I have to say that it was a thoroughly enjoyable period of time. Rarely in academic life do we now have the opportunity to stop and think about one thing really deeply – our lives as academics are pulled every which way, divided between teaching, research and service, in which, even ring-fencing a full day to spend on scholarly activity becomes a rare luxury. So, the sabbatical, for me, was time to focus on one thing and one thing only – the architecture of the visitor centre. And in doing so, I realised that it is a far richer topic than I had initially thought. As well as the topics I'd initially thought it would focus on (place, context and the first-time visitor) others such as meaning, empathy, landscape, setting, typology, archetypes, experience, authenticity, iconicity etc. all became increasingly relevant.

Another part of the journey behind this book, which has been very special for me, has been the story behind the photographs. When I started out, it was clear to me that what we needed to do was to hire a professional architectural photographer to re-visit and re-photograph all of the visitor centres featured in the book. When this proved to be beyond our budget, a number of options were mooted, the most improbable (in my mind) was that I would end up taking the photographs. Again, this is where Valerie Rose has had a strong hand in shaping the book. Having seen some of the photographs that I had already taken when visiting some of the first

visitor centres, she encouraged me to carry on taking the photographs to be used in this book and this is an aspect to writing the book that has proved surprisingly fulfilling. There is certainly something about the act of photographing a building that is quantifiably different to simply visiting it and looking at it. I know that I look at buildings in a different way, as an architect, compared to non-architects, but I am now clear that I look at buildings differently when photographing them (and differently when again sketching them). The act of looking at something, for an extended period of time (whether photographing or sketching), is incomparably valuable and, as a consequence, the act of writing and the act of photographing start to blend together (and this is an activity that I hope to certainly continue in the future). This is also something for which I have to thank Valerie.

In addition to this, I have benefitted greatly from discussions with colleagues and fellow academics (and the students of course, as mentioned already). Previous drafts of this work have been considerably improved and criticised by many of them and I owe a great debt to all of the following: Ermal Shpuza, for his advice on the analysis of morphological shapes (which I undertook although sadly this analysis is not incorporated into the final version of the book); David Seamon, for his advice on the phenomenological interpretation of place and for reading and commenting on draft chapters; Susan Ashley, for conversations about visitor centres, talking to me about her personal experiences of working in them and for reading and commenting on the draft chapters; Tom Mordue (the Norman Richardson Professor of Tourism, Newcastle Business School), for further conversations about visitor centres and for also reading and commenting on draft chapters and Paul Jones, for discussions on the architectural design aspects of visitor centres and for his prescience in setting the two MArch 'live projects' focusing on visitor centres, mentioned above.

In addition to the above, invaluable inputs to the text, I would also like to acknowledge (in no particular order): Amelia and Aidan Dalton, for accompanying me on so many of my visits (and to whom this book is dedicated); The Northumbria

University MArch students for their inspiring work on The Land of Oak & Iron Heritage Centre and The Angel of the North Visitor Centre and for asking all the right challenging questions; Dean Ireland and Clare O'Connell (Northumbria University MArch students), for redrawing all the plans into single house style; Sarah Loveland (of Sarah Loveland Photography), for her photographic advice; Glen McHale, John Woodward and the Faculty Sabbatical Committee, for granting me sabbatical leave to complete this work; Thora Tenbrink, for letting me stay with her when I went to visit Snowdon and being patient with an unplanned and extended visit when the weather just wouldn't cooperate with my plans; Rosi Jelfs, for her assistance with the literature review; all the members of Hadrian Clog, for making the experience of visiting Whitby Abbey visitor centre a particularly special and memorable one; visitors and guides of all the visitor centres – but one in particular stands out, Gordon Campbell, for his superb knowledge and expertise about the Titan Crane; Danilo di Mascio, for his help in the last six weeks of the book, without which I would have been unable to meet the deadline, due to other (unforeseen) commitments; to Stuart Evans, Alison Thornton-Sykes, Ivor Crowther, Val Gibson and Ian Jackson – for giving up their valuable time to be interviewed about The Sill visitor centre; Valerie Rose – for the opportunity to work on this book and for her ongoing support; To the many architectural practices with whom I have been in contact – for making this book happen and for being so cooperative and supportive during the process of writing it.

And last, but not least, to Nick 'Sheep' Dalton – for his patience and support, particularly during these last few months, when I have been trying to combine finishing the book with being Head of Department (the unforeseen commitment).

As usual, any mistakes or errors are mine and mine alone.

Introduction

The main goal of this book is to produce the definitive book on the architecture of the visitor centre. In recent years some incredible, architecturally significant visitor centres have been designed and built, and this book provides the first opportunity to bring these together under a single publication. The original contribution to the academic discipline of architecture made by this book is that it is the first study conducted to bring together, document and analyse this relatively new building type (and answer the important question of whether it can be considered a new building type).

This book is geographically set in the United Kingdom, meaning England, Scotland, Wales and Northern Ireland. In the process of writing this book, I travelled as far north as Inverness (the Culloden Battlefield and visitor centre), as far south as Portsmouth (The Mary Rose Museum and visitor centre), as far east as Ipswich (the Sutton Hoo visitor centre) and as far west as the Giant's Causeway in Northern Ireland. All visits took place between January and December 2016 (and all travel, expenses and equipment were paid for by Northumbria University). Although this book happens to focus on those visitor centres located in the UK (for ease of access: it would have been impossible to have visited a sufficient number of visitor centres, in such a short period of time, had I had to factor in the additional time required for international travel), the proliferation of high quality, architecturally significant visitor centres, built in recent years, is not a phenomenon peculiar to this country. Indeed, it could certainly be considered an international phenomenon, since noteworthy visitor centres outside the UK include, in particular, the Domkyrkoforum, Lund, Sweden by Carmen Izquierdo Arkitektkontor, an urban visitor centre in a sensitive historic location and the Pannonhalma Abdij Visitor Centre built in 2010 by Roeleveld-Sikkes. Unlike the urban Domkyrkoforum visitor centre, the Pannonhalma is in a rural location in the grounds of a Benedictine monastery. Other recent, notable international examples include the Lascaux IV visitor centre by Snøhetta and Duncan Lewis Scape Architecture in France; the Wadden Sea Centre in Denmark by Dorte Mandrup Arkitekter; the Visitor Center of the Roman Theatre of Malaga by Tejedor Linares & asociados; the visitor centre at Heidelberg Castle by Max Dudler Architekt in Germany; the Trollstigen Visitor Center, by Reiulf Ramstad Architects in Norway; the Allmannajuvet Zinc Mine Museum by Peter Zumthor, also in Norway; the Korean Island visitor centre, by OUJAE Architects; the Cairns Botanic Gardens Visitors Centre / Charles Wright Architects in Australia; the Jianamani Visitor Center, by Atelier TeamMinus in China and M-Arquitectos's visitor centre at the Thermal Springs Pools Poça da Dona Beija, São Miguel Island, Portugal. If this book succeeds in explaining why this, potentially new, building type has recently become so prevalent, then this rationale is likely to apply equally as well to the international examples cited above, as to the British buildings featured in this book.

In chronological terms, what is so interesting about the visitor centre as a building 'type' is that it is a relative newcomer (fascinating, in its own right), and as yet does not exist in most classifications or taxonomies of building types (such as the UK government's planning use classes). The visitor centre is functionally related to the information centre, the cafe and to the museum, but this publication will focus solely on architectural examples that are unequivocally examples of the 'new' visitor centre and not on other closely related, yet different, building types. Of all the examples of visitor centres in this book, none pre-date the early 1990s. It is therefore proposed that the chronological scope of this book is from 1990 to the present day. The focus is on completed projects, but there are a few projects currently under construction that are due for completion (or will be close to completion) in the next twelve months, and therefore have been included.

For the most part, the sample of visitor centres in this publication has focused on those buildings that have been nominated for, or have won, architectural awards or were architectural competition winners (as a proxy for 'quality'). In terms of numbers, the aim of this publication was to study, in detail, 20 exemplar buildings, which are included as 'mini-chapters' in the second part of the book. However, in order to identify these 20 exemplars, a far wider set of buildings needed to be visited, documented and analysed and it is this wider set of buildings that forms the context for the first four chapters of the book, which tackle the questions of what is a visitor centre? What is the relationship between visitor centre and landscape/place? And what is the role of the visitor?

In the course of researching this book, 43 buildings were studied and, where possible, visited (a small number of buildings had yet to be built, were closed for refurbishment or had recently closed and therefore not all were able to be visited). All the buildings were photographed, and the architects were contacted to provide drawings and a 'key facts' data sheet. (Almost all the architects contacted cooperated generously with this project). The drawings were subsequently re-drawn and spatially analysed (primarily using space syntax methods).

The names and locations of the visitor centres included in the book can be seen on the map in Figure 0.1.

In addition to the site visits described above, a series of in-depth interviews with a range of stakeholders for a specific, single visitor centre, were conducted. This visitor centre is The Sill visitor centre, which is currently under construction, close to Hadrian's Wall in the Northumberland National Park. Given that one of the largest and most ambitious visitors' centres to have been built recently, is so close to completion, and has had so many people thinking hard about the kinds of questions that have been asked in this book (What is a visitor centre? What does it do? What should it look like? What should its relationship to the landscape be like?), it seemed worthwhile to try to capture some of this while these thoughts were still fresh in people's minds. As part of the research for this book, therefore, a set of interviews were conducted with several key stakeholders involved in The Sill project. Excerpts from these interviews have been included in the first part of the book.

The interviewees consist of:

The Funder: Ivor Crowther, Head of the Heritage Lottery Fund in the North East. Since the Heritage Lottery Fund for this project provided a substantial amount of money for 'The Sill', they can be regarded as one of its primary funders.

The Client: Stuart Evans, Head of Corporate Services at the Northumberland National Park Authority and a member of the Authority's Executive Leadership Team. Stuart has been most closely involved in the day-to-day oversight of the project.

The Architect: Alison Thornton-Sykes is Principal Architect at JDDK Architects and Project Architect for The Sill Landscape Discovery Centre. She has recently worked on two other visitor centres, RSPB Saltholme (completed in 2009) and the planned RSPB Sherwood Forest visitor centre.

The Local Farmer and Parish Councillor: Val Gibson, a local farmer whose family has lived on her farm (with views of The Whin Sill) for five generations and who took part in many of the participatory/community events run by the Northumberland National Park Authority and JDDK Architects.

The Neighbour/Geologist: Ian Jackson, the nearest residential neighbour to The Sill visitor centre, and whose house has unobstructed views to the new building. He is also a retired geologist and has a keen interest in the geological story behind 'The Sill'. Like Val Gibson, he took part in many of the participatory design and community consultation events that have taken place.

In this first section, the key theoretical ideas behind this building type will also be presented and discussed and in Chapter 4, a case will be made for

visitor centres being a new building type and an 'archetypal' visitor centre is described; this chapter marks the conclusion of the theoretical part of the book. In the second part, 20 exemplar visitor centres are presented and the experience of visiting them is described. They have been selected to show the widest possible range of sizes (from the largest and most costly to the smallest and least expensive), of ages (from the oldest at 25 years, to one on the cusp of being opened) and the greatest range of locations and of attraction types/themes.

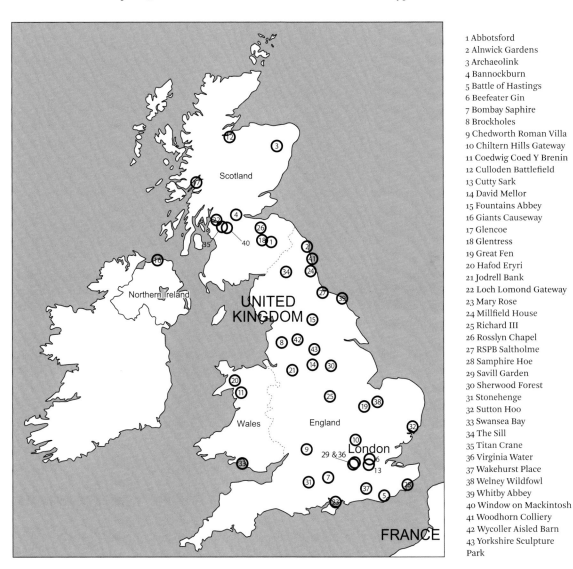

1 Abbotsford
2 Alnwick Gardens
3 Archaeolink
4 Bannockburn
5 Battle of Hastings
6 Beefeater Gin
7 Bombay Saphire
8 Brockholes
9 Chedworth Roman Villa
10 Chiltern Hills Gateway
11 Coedwig Coed Y Brenin
12 Culloden Battlefield
13 Cutty Sark
14 David Mellor
15 Fountains Abbey
16 Giants Causeway
17 Glencoe
18 Glentress
19 Great Fen
20 Hafod Eryri
21 Jodrell Bank
22 Loch Lomond Gateway
23 Mary Rose
24 Millfield House
25 Richard III
26 Rosslyn Chapel
27 RSPB Saltholme
28 Samphire Hoe
29 Savill Garden
30 Sherwood Forest
31 Stonehenge
32 Sutton Hoo
33 Swansea Bay
34 The Sill
35 Titan Crane
36 Virginia Water
37 Wakehurst Place
38 Welney Wildfowl
39 Whitby Abbey
40 Window on Mackintosh
41 Woodhorn Colliery
42 Wycoller Aisled Barn
43 Yorkshire Sculpture Park

Figure 0.1 Locations of the visitor centres

1.
What is a Visitor Centre?

What could be more fitting, when starting a book on the architecture of visitor centres, than to ask the (seemingly) simple question of *what exactly is a visitor centre?*

Only a generation ago, any architect or student of architecture picking up a reference book of planning and design data (The *Metric Handbook* or Neufert's *Architects' Data* to name but two examples) would be confronted with sections on how to plan and spatially lay out any number of building 'types': offices, museums, restaurants, houses etc., but they would certainly not have found a single reference to a visitor centre. Of course, entries on a visitor centre's constituent parts would have been included (the museum/gallery, the cafe/restaurant, the shop and public toilets) but the highly specialised building that we are coming to recognise as the modern visitor centre, would not have been listed as a type and neither would the term have featured anywhere in such design guidance.

This is actually quite exciting. A tantalising thought hangs in the air before us, 'could this actually be a new building type?' And why, exactly, might this be exciting? Well, building types are relatively stable: they tend not to burst suddenly on to the architectural scene and, as a consequence, most building types have been around for centuries, if not longer. Furthermore, if there are changes, they tend to be minor trends or variations on existing types – for example, the growth in single occupancy dwellings versus large family houses. As a trend in housing, these are nuanced changes in a robust and

established type, rather than an entirely new type per se. Therefore, *if* the visitor centre is actually a new building type, this is our first chance to attempt to capture its essence, to document and to define it (rather like a Victorian lepidopterist spotting a new variety of butterfly).

In order to determine whether or not visitor centres might be a new architectural 'type', or not, the theory of building types needs first to be briefly described. It feels as though the concept of 'type' should be intuitively simple (after all, a house is a house and clearly quite different from a church, which is, unarguably, a church, and factories are obviously entirely different buildings again … see Figure 1.1 for a clichéd view of building types by the architectural cartoonist, Louis Hellman). In architecture, a taxonomic classification of a building's (usually physical) characteristics is known as 'typology'. The concept of a building type can be traced back to the eighteenth century and the work of Quatremère de Quincy. He suggested that, 'the word "type" presents less the image of a thing

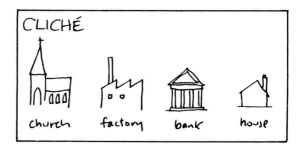

Figure 1.1 A clichéd view of building types by Louis Hellman
Source: Louis Hellman, used with permission

to copy or imitate completely than the idea of an element which ought itself to serve as the rule for a model' (Quatremère de Quincy, 1825). In other words, the idea of a specific building type (be it a house, church, factory or, indeed, a visitor centre) is not something ever to be found in the real world but rather exists as an abstracted ideal, a reified model, to which all other real-world instances can be compared and found to match to a greater or lesser degree. It is as if every time we look at a building, for example, a house, we are mentally comparing it to our 'back catalogue' of every house we have ever seen, been inside or read about. By doing so, we *somehow* arrive at the judgement that the example in front of us, bears sufficient similarity to the totality of all other examples we have ever experienced in order to be deemed the same. At this point, we can conclude that we really are looking at a 'house' (or insert 'other building type' here). The question of what it is that we are looking for when we make such a judgement clearly lies at the heart of this activity, but this is something that momentarily needs to be put to one side (but will be shortly revisited), in order to ask one final, interesting question. If assigning a specific instance of a building to an abstract category of type depends on comparing it to all other instances that have gone before, how can this be possible for a potentially new building type where only a few, or even no, examples exist? In other words, how do new building types arise?

Giulio Carlo Argan in his book chapter, 'On the Typology of Architecture', asks exactly the same question of how an architectural type comes into existence. He states unequivocally that type 'is never formulated *a priori* but always deduced from a series of instances' (Argan, 1963/1996, p. 243). And he goes on to say, 'The birth of a 'type' is therefore dependent on the existence of a series of buildings having between them an obvious formal and functional analogy' (ibid., p. 243). Therefore, an individual building cannot be declared the first example of a new type; sufficient numbers of such buildings must be built and then examined retrospectively in order to determine if a new building type might have come into existence. This seems to make intuitive sense, and certainly fits with the description above as to

what it is we are doing when we assign a building to a type. We can clearly only do this if a sufficient number, a critical mass of examples, already exist with which to make a comparison. The question of how many prior examples are enough to make such a judgement is something that has seldom, if ever, been discussed in architectural theory, but to answer this, simple statistics may be used for guidance. For any sample size (in this case, numbers of buildings, but it could be anything) we can calculate a 'margin of error' in order to determine whether we have sufficient buildings to say anything meaningful. For 43 buildings (the number that has been researched for this book) the margin of error is about 15 per cent (Niles, 2006). Whether this is sufficient margin of error depends on the wider context of the study (as well as the risks of getting it wrong), but in this case, 15 per cent possible error seems about right.

So what is it that people are looking at when they make a judgement that a building is an example of a specific type? In Argan's quote above he provides some clues as he mentions the need to look for both formal and functional analogies between a set of buildings, in order to identify a common type. This is akin to saying that every dog I have ever seen has four legs and a tail (the formal analogy) and chases balls (the functional analogy) therefore, I can conclude that anything else I might encounter in the future with four legs, a tail, and chasing a ball is *probably* (remember the margin of error) a dog. It also means that if I meet a three-legged, ball-chasing, tail-wagging dog, I am still able to recognise the strong degree of correspondence with our ideal model, and determine that this may well be another example of a dog, albeit a somewhat unusual one.

We now have formal and functional analogies (in order to establish a building type), to which a third category of analogies might be usefully added, namely spatial analogies. In *Space is the Machine*, Bill Hillier suggests that in architecture, the way that we notice similarities between buildings of the same type is through their *spatial configuration*. By this he means how a building's interior spaces and rooms are interconnected, the sequence in which its functional or named-spaces are encountered or experienced and the overall spatial pattern thus created. In space syntax theory, houses are identifiable as instances of a single type precisely because of such observed, spatial commonalities. For example, in most houses, in most cultures, the first space entered from the outside is typically some kind of entry-space, hall or circulation-space connected to a reception room into which guests may be brought. In other words, reception rooms are typically the most public spaces in a house, are spatially close to the outside; a visitor can be welcomed into this space without having to pass through too many other domestic spaces or rooms. Conversely, bedrooms are typically the 'deepest' spaces in the house, the furthest (in terms of spatial connections) from the outside and hence the most private. By analysing a large number of houses as networks of connected spaces, these commonalities can be identified and a building type defined. Therefore, spatial analogies may also be added to the list of tests for any new building type.

Before we can establish whether or not the visitor centre is a new 'type' (formally, functionally and spatially), we might usefully start by defining what *is* a visitor centre and what it *does*.

What is the Purpose of a Visitor Centre?

A good way to begin is with the long-held tradition of defining something by defining *what it is not*. As touched upon briefly above, one way of regarding a visitor centre is to consider its constituent parts. Of the 43 British visitor centres researched for this book (please refer to the introduction for the scope of the buildings studied) they can be analysed as having the following mix of constituent parts: approximately 70 per cent of all visitor centres contain a cafe or restaurant, shop and toilets. 67 per cent of visitor centres contain a dedicated exhibition area, in contrast to, for example, 14 per cent of visitor centres that contain a gallery, etc. (See Figure 1.2). This mix of functions is at the heart of visitor centres, as Ian Jackson, nearest neighbour to The Sill visitor centre (and participant in the stakeholder interviews), observed:

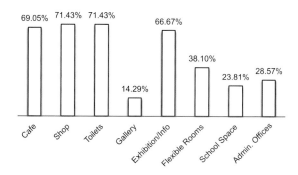

Figure 1.2 **The proportion of all visitor centres containing different functional spaces**

Visitor centres have kind of expanded, almost exploded. In themselves they're great and wonderful opportunities to do all those things: keep people fed, watered, keep them dry in winter [and] when this place [the Northumberland National Park] is like it was this morning, give them some little seed [of knowledge] that just might grow, or raise their curiosity and get them outside.

So perhaps we can consider the purpose of a visitor centre by considering, in turn, the purposes of these most frequently encountered sub-spaces. For example: the purpose of a *museum* is to bring together collections of objects and display them for education and entertainment; the purpose of a *shop* is to exchange goods/services with customers for money; the purpose of a *cafe* is to provide sustenance in the form of light snacks and, typically, hot beverages (and where the key aim is 're-fuelling'); the purpose of a *restaurant* is to provide fine dining in the form of a wider selection of food, typically of more than one course (and where the key aim is the overall 'sensual experience'); the purpose of *public toilets* are to serve a universal biological need in a clean and private environment; the purpose of an *office* is for employees to undertake administrative tasks, etc. So, can these definitions perhaps be merged and it be suggested that the purpose of a visitor centre is to *display items for education and entertainment whilst simultaneously exchanging goods for money, providing sustenance and serving other biological needs*? As definitions go, this is patently absurd on many levels. Therefore, let us abandon this route and go back to basics: Is the purpose of a visitor centre, more simply, *to facilitate the act of visiting*? This seems a far more existential purpose than the rigidly functional (and ridiculous) definition above. But here is the nub of the question, is the former definition simply a more verbose version of the latter one, or is it quintessentially different in some manner? Perhaps another way of posing this question is to ask whether a visitor centre is more than the sum of its parts. In a series of interviews with stakeholders for the new visitor centre in Northumbria National Park, The Sill, the Principal Architect at JDDK Architects and Project Architect for The Sill Landscape Discovery Centre, Alison Thornton-Sykes, observed:

> I think [the visitor centre] is very much more than the sum of the parts. I think what's been consistent in the ones that I've worked with is that it's much more about engaging the visitor in the subject of that visitor centre. So, for example the RSPB [Saltholme visitor centre], is about engaging people, exciting people, inspiring them about wildlife, and in the case of 'The Sill', it's really about engaging people, and inspiring them, and educating them about landscape: a springboard, really. It's the starting point for people to then go off and discover more. While it does house all the practical considerations of cafe, retail and toilet facilities, as well as [an] exhibition, I think it's much more than that. It's much more about providing that springboard, about appealing to a wider audience.

It is clear that Alison Thornton-Sykes thinks that visitor centres are certainly more than the sum of their constituent parts, but how do we take this further?

In order to explore this line of inquiry there is a need to establish what a visitor centre *is* or what it *does* (and then to see whether these map onto the functions of the sub-spaces, as described above, or whether visitor centres are and do more than this). It can be suggested that there are several characteristics that make a visitor centre a visitor centre and not, for example, a museum (its closest typological relative). One question that was frequently encountered, when researching this book, was whether the visitor centre was simply a museum under a new name. And if not a traditional nineteenth/twentieth-century museum, is it perhaps no more than a recently evolved, nuanced variation of the museum type. After all, in Don Thompson's paper presenting an architectural view of the experience of museums, he describes the evolution of the museum from the private collection to the classical, reverence-inspiring temple of the arts and sciences and then to the modern, 'more innovative … museum … radiat[ing] wonder and intrigue' (Thompson, 1991, p. 73). If we accept that museums have already been evolving over the centuries, is it not feasible, even highly probable, that the visitor centre of today could perhaps be nothing more than a recent stage in this well-established process of museums adapting to societal and cultural change?

This individual question should be considered separately as it is important. After much consideration, I would like to begin by suggesting that the first examination of whether or not a visitor centre is a museum, is to ask the following question: can the visitor centre be geographically re-located elsewhere? I would like to state that I believe that the visitor centre is inextricably bound to its physical place and location in the landscape (so much so that the entire next chapter will be devoted to the relationship between visitor centres and place), in a way that museums need not be. It is nonsensical to imagine (as a thought experiment) the Stonehenge visitor centre being located in Birmingham or The Sill visitor centre in Central London. Culloden and Bannockburn visitor centres (sites of famous Scottish battles), could not conceivably be placed anywhere south of the Scottish border. Whereas in contrast, any number of cities may, and frequently do, have a science museum, museum of childhood or a natural history museum etc., and so this assessment of 'relocatability' should be the first evaluative criterion that

Figure 1.3 The welcoming environment at the summit of Snowdon

could be applied, when trying to discern whether a building is visitor centre or is a museum.

The second criterion is more of a heuristic one, but one that is both worth mentioning and worth asking of the building: which came first: the attraction or the visitor centre? For the most part, visitors were *already* visiting (the 'attraction') and visitor centres are constructed to render what the general public are already doing, more pleasant, comfortable or amenable (i.e. *to facilitate the act of visiting*, to revisit our statement from the previous section). Only a very small proportion of the visitor centres referenced in this book were designed to attract people to a hitherto unvisited site rather than to accommodate people who were already coming. In other words, the situation where the visitor centre was built to promote and raise awareness about a new attraction is the exception rather than the rule. For the most part, the 'attraction' was already there and the visitors were already coming. A good example of this is Ray Hole Architects' visitor centre at the summit of Snowdon; people do not climb to the top of Snowdon simply because there is a new visitor centre there; people have been climbing the mountain for centuries. However, since the construction of the new visitor centre, their experience of arriving at the summit has been rendered far more comfortable and welcoming (see Figure 1.3).

The next question to ask, in order to distinguish a visitor centre from a museum, is whether the primary motivation of the visitors to the building is to 'acquire knowledge' or to 'have an experience'. It can be suggested that if visitors are aiming to do the former (i.e. acquire knowledge), then the building is more likely to be a museum but if they are hoping to achieve the latter (to have an experience) then the building is probably a visitor centre. The visitor perspective will be explored more fully in Chapter 3.

And finally, since many (67 per cent) visitor centres do contain some kind of exhibition or information area, we can ask the following question of the exhibits contained: are the exhibits housed in the building or around the site of a more or less *equivalent* importance or status, or are they dominated by one single, typically large 'exhibit' or 'resource'? To be clear, I am counting the Stonehenge monument, the entirety of Hadrian's Wall and the geological phenomenon, which is The Whin Sill and the mountain of Snowdon as 'exhibits' or 'resources' in the context of this question. Although the archetypal visitor centre may contain a small collection of exhibits these are clearly secondary to (or explanatory of) the main attraction itself. See Figure 1.4 for a diagrammatic representation of this difference between a museum and a visitor centre.

It is worth noting that the spatial relationship between the visitor centre and its main 'exhibit' or attraction can vary considerably. It may be fully enclosed inside the building, in the case of the *Mary Rose* which has been entirely enveloped by its visitor centre or the Chedworth Roman Villa visitor centre

(A in Figure 1.5), it may be semi-enclosed, as in the Cutty Sark visitor centre (B, see also the book's frontispiece), adjacent or touching, as in the Rosslyn Chapel visitor centre (C), next to or close by, as in the Titan Crane or the 'Window on Mackintosh' visitor centres (D) or located at quite some distance away, as in the Giant's Causeway, Fountains Abbey or Stonehenge visitor centres (E) or finally, the 'attraction' may completely surround the visitor centre, as in the example of the visitor centre at the summit of Snowdon (F). Figure 1.5 illustrates graphically the possible set of relationships between the visitor centre and its main attraction. Returning to Alison Thornton-Sykes, Project Architect of The Sill visitor centre, she observes:

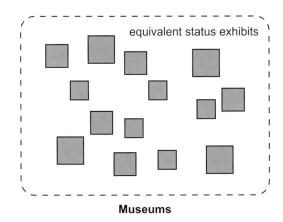

Museums

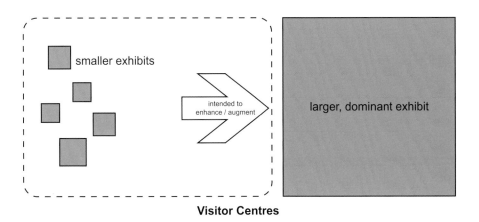

Visitor Centres

Figure 1.4 A comparison between museums and visitor centres

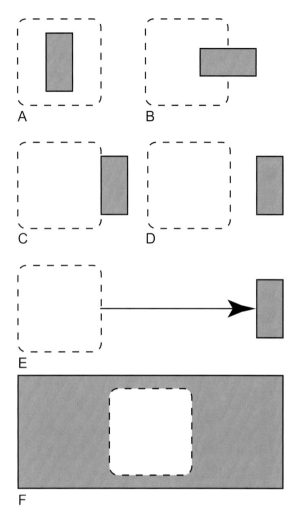

A. Attraction inside the visitor centre
B. Attraction semi-enclosed by the visitor centre
C. Attraction adjacent/touching the visitor centre
D. Attraction near to the visitor centre
E. Attraction distant from the visitor centre
F. Visitor centre surrounded by the attraction

Figure 1.5 Spatial relationship of visitor centre to the main attraction or resource (grey = attraction or resource; dashed line = external envelope of the visitor centre)

Architecture plays an important part in [changing people]. It has to latch onto what the client's aspirations are about exciting and inspiring people, and the architecture has to tell that story. I think the interpretation and exhibition does that to an extent, as well, and [it is] how [the exhibits and the building] interact together. It's very much that the building is the exhibition, in a way, and the interpretation is fully integrated, not just in the exhibition hall, but also in the reception and the cafe [and] on the roof, so the roof experience [in The Sill] is part of that interpretation.

In which case, according to Thornton-Sykes, the visitor centre and the exhibition, ideally, start to merge to become one and the same (or at the very least, the distinction between them starts to become somewhat fuzzy).

To summarise, it can be suggested that the four key criteria for distinguishing visitor centres from museums are:

1. The visitor centre cannot be located elsewhere (the sense of place is central);
2. The 'attraction' and the presence of visitors typically (although not always) predate the construction of the visitor centre;
3. The main purpose of a visitor centre is 'having an experience' rather than 'acquiring knowledge' (as in a museum);
4. Its exhibits, if it has any, are frequently not equivalent in status, as one 'exhibit' (i.e. the main attraction) tends to significantly dominate the visiting experience.

These criteria need not all be met to justify it being classified as a visitor centre, but it could be suggested that, ideally, three of the four criteria should be met. In this section, the differences between the museum, and the visitor centre, as distinct building types have been established; we can now, therefore, move on to define what a visitor centre is in its own right: why it exists? what it does? and how does it do it?

The Why, What and How of Visitor Centres

It could be suggested that a visitor centre is not absolutely essential to any visitor site but rather it can play a crucial role in contributing to the experience and understanding of the main attraction or resource. There are a number of fairly straightforward ways that a visitor centre can do this and they can be enumerated:

1. Awareness-raising
2. Portal and orientation
3. Education
4. Experience framing
5. Belonging and place-enhancing
6. Guiding or controlling movement
7. Attraction protection
8. Income generation

This first purpose, that of awareness raising, serves as an umbrella for the next four activities on this list; the awareness-raising is actualised through the 'portal and orientation', 'education', 'framing of experiences' and the 'place-making' functions. Of the final three items, those of 'guiding or controlling movement' and 'protecting the attraction' are also strongly connected. Finally, the purpose of 'income generation' rather stands outside these other seven activities, but can be important (especially for a client considering whether or not to build one). The final section of this chapter will briefly discuss these eight roles in turn.

Awareness-raising

Before a visitor has even arrived at the building, it can perform a function even 'at a distance' since it can have an awareness-raising role. Even if the attraction is of a long-standing duration and if people have already been visiting the site (one of the four suggested tests of a visitor centre) the creation of a new visitor centre can stimulate or renew interest in, and generally promote, the location and its concomitant attraction. A new facility can also serve to expand or widen an existing set of visitors, so that new people, or even a new generation of visitors, are inspired, enabled or encouraged to visit.

Portal and Orientation

Upon arrival, the building can act as a portal or a gateway to an attraction. As such it both welcomes as well as provides a starting point for the overall visiting experience. This gateway can be a literal one, particularly if tickets are required to enter the site (in which case the 'portal' serves as a spatial control mechanism that must be negotiated and successfully passed through in order to access the site beyond; in this scenario the visitor centre staff are not merely enablers of the visit but are the gatekeepers of it). Conversely, the gateway may be symbolic, simply marking the start (and possibly also the end point) of the visit. Ian Jackson, neighbour of The Sill visitor centre, describes this 'portal' aspect of visitor centres:

> In a sense, if it works properly, [the visitor centre] could be a little like the wardrobe in *The Lion, the Witch and the Wardrobe*: it might just be a portal to everything else. It would be great if this place just produced a few children who said, 'Yes, I'm curious about that.' That's the opportunity it loses if it doesn't get it right, so that's what I think a visitor centre should do.

Ivor Crowther, the Head of the Heritage Lottery Fund in the North East, and one of the primary funders of The Sill visitor centre (and hence also one of the participants in the stakeholder interviews), provides a very powerful vision of the building-as-portal: 'I think our current Chief Executive describes The Sill as the "iPad for the landscape". It's a way that people will learn to discover the landscape, be it using it as an educational journey or just using it as a way to get in and find information.'

Where the attraction is located at some distance from the visitor centre (category 'D' in Figure 1.5) the ritual of 'arrival' is only the start of a possibly lengthy process of reaching the attraction itself. Ivor Crowther (Heritage Lottery Fund), when asked about the aspects of good design that they, as the funder, are looking for, was clear that 'there's that sense of arrival that you need to get right.' When a visitor approaches a site, and is perhaps following a path to get there, they will naturally anticipate both events and possible actions along the route and their subsequent arrival. For architects, such anticipation is something to be encouraged; the idea prevails that a heightened sense of anticipation will make the act of approaching a site more pleasurable. Philip Johnson observes, 'It is known to the veriest tourist how much more he enjoys the Parthenon because he has to walk up the Acropolis [and] how much less he enjoys Chartres Cathedral because he is unceremoniously dumped in front of it' (Johnson, 1965, p. 168). Equally, Philip Thiel refers to such anticipation as a 'future experience' (Thiel, 1997) and highlights its importance as a criterion for judging the performance of public buildings and spaces. Therefore, it is important to remember that the 'portal' function of a visitor centre may be more *immediate* or more *prolonged* depending upon the spatial relationship between the building and the attraction.

Education

Despite the previously mentioned test as to whether the building is primarily intended to support the *acquiring of knowledge* or *having an experience*, there undoubtedly remains an educational role for visitor centres (and this is precisely why it can be so difficult to distinguish them from museums), even if it is subordinate to its experiential role. A visitor centre enables the visitor to learn more about the attraction and its spatial, historical, environmental or even commercial context. This learning role is not separate to the building's role in helping to create an experience, since one provides the context and background information for the other. The two can exist apart but in reality, each serves to enrich the other.

Alison Thornton-Sykes, Project Architect, describes the way in which The Sill visitor centre has already been raising awareness and serving an educational function, even though it is not yet completed.

For [The Heritage Lottery Fund], one of their main priorities is about the educational aspects, and how it's going to reach out to a community, and to younger people. And that's right through the commissioning of the project, through the development of the design. So, we've all had student work placements. We've been heavily involved with the Northumbria and Newcastle universities and the students there. So, the building, in its own right, has become an educational programme. But it's much [more] about the activities programme that's going to be going on in this building, and what the building's going to be housing, and how it can outreach, as well, because it's for the Northumberland National Park. This is just a gateway, really, to the wider National Park, and [the] wider landscape beyond. The building is a means to an end, in a way, of housing a starting point for all these activities.

Experience Framing

The next purpose of the visitor centre to be discussed is that of 'framing' an experience (after Basil Bernstein, 1975). Our experience of visiting somewhere is 'framed' by the selection of what the visitor is exposed to and also the sequencing and pacing of this material ('Framing' is usually used in the context of pedagogic theory but can equally be applied to framing the visiting experience). In the case of visitor centres the act of framing is controlled by both the building's spatial design and the selection of any educational material housed within it. The idea that the sequence and pacing of objects or exhibits, spaces, views, other information etc. encountered during a visit help to frame the visitors' experience is strongly related to two other concepts in architecture. The first of these is the idea of narrative. Narrative in architecture is defined as the meaning/storytelling derived from the spatial sequencing of information encountered by someone moving through a building (see, in particular, Psarra, 2009 and Coates, 2012). Described in this way, the majority of visitor centres can clearly be held to be strong narrative-buildings. The second concept that is also associated with the way in which the visitor centre engenders the experience of the visitor is through the performance-related terms of 'theatre' and 'staging'. The information encountered by a visitor can be curated and staged by both the spatial layout of the building and by the placement of exhibits within it. Furthermore, the way in which information or objects are staged can even directly affect a visitor's sense of authenticity of place, as described by MacCannell on this topic (1973). It is clear that these concepts of experience creation and curation, framing, staging and narrative are all strongly bound together and are undoubtedly one of the primary purposes of the visitor centre.

Since we have already touched on the concept of curating the visitor experience via the sequence of paths taken through the visitor centre, then another obvious purpose of the design of the visitor centre building is to guide or control (depending on the degree of freedom permitted) the paths, routes and orientation of the visitors through the site. More control might be exercised if particular routes or sequences of paths are intended to be followed or if visitor numbers (perhaps to a fragile attraction) need to be restricted. The circulation paths might be interior routes inside the visitor centre building, or they might negotiate a larger, exterior site.

Belonging and Place-enhancing

Another function that visitor centres might have is to help visitors forge a connection with a specific place. The first suggested characteristic of a visitor centre, as presented in the previous section of this chapter, was its lack of 'relocatability' and therefore an emphasis on there being a strong relationship between the building and place can already be inferred. The kinds of places where visitor centres are built tend to be locations that already have a strong sense of place, indeed they are often 'exceptional places' (Relph, 2008), for example, Stonehenge or the Giant's Causeway, but perhaps the role of the visitor centre might be to help hone or amplify this sense of place. In just the same way that a lens can focus light to a point, so may a well-designed visitor centre help focus our personal sense of place and of belonging. The role of architecture in 'place-making' is again a common theme in modern architectural theory, as is contextualism to which it is related. It can be suggested that they differ: contextualism is about the building belonging or responding to its context whereas the building as a mechanism of place-making (or place-enhancing) is about using the building to help us feel we belong and it is the

latter that well designed visitor centres can aspire to do. The idea that place and landscape are of utmost importance to visitor centres will be discussed more fully in the next chapter.

Guiding Movement and Attraction Protection

Another role that a visitor centre might play is of protecting access to an attraction. As mentioned above, routes to, and numbers of pedestrians moving through, a site might need to be controlled as part of the overall circulation and protection strategy. In the more extreme cases, the building itself might need to serve as a replacement or substitute for the attraction itself, if the attraction is particularly fragile or vulnerable. In this case the visitor centre is not only acting in a protective role (a role which might be its predominant one) but a symbolic, representative (as a stand-in) one too.

Income Generation

Finally, the last purpose that a visitor centre might be considered to have is that of income generation. (Although, for a client putting together a business case for a new visitor centre this will more likely be their first consideration). Where a steady number of visitors have already been coming to a site, the increased income that a new building could stimulate might be about simply increasing visitor numbers or it might be about helping to maximise income via secondary outlets such as food or souvenir retail. Ivor Crowther, of the Heritage Lottery Fund, was keen to stress the wider opportunities associated with a new visitor centre. 'The development of the business side, the business hook, which will operate from [The Sill visitor centre] as well, gives lots of opportunities that weren't there, as well'. The client for The Sill, Stuart Evans, Head of Corporate Services at the Northumberland National Park Authority, also talked (in the stakeholder interviews) about the importance of getting the business case and the numbers of predicted visitors right:

Size matters, in terms of getting it right, not just for now but for future visitors, because if we take 100,000 people a year over 100 years, that's

10 million. As the client you have responsibility for immediate customers but also you have a responsibility for the future. You've got a responsibility for different people in society. You've also got responsibility for people as they age and as their families age. If there are a group of eight people going out, [and] if one of them has a mobility issue, preventing them from visiting, that means eight people don't go, not one. That was very important to us.

In the minority case where there has been no past history of visitors prior to the visitor centre being built (the Titan Crane in Glasgow is an example of this: the crane itself existed but it did not actively promote visitors prior to having a visitor centre) then the creation of a visitor centre can be about encouraging people to the site and generating income where in the past there has been none (see Figure 1.6). Ivor Crowther, of the Heritage Lottery Fund, was keen to stress the importance of getting the business case right:

> I think sometimes, we see quite a lot of visitor centres. In the North East we have not funded a great number of visitor centres. We'll only agree to a heritage centre or visitor centre if it's needed, if it can be justified, and if it can be sustained. We don't have projects that fall over because, within two years' time, people have lost interest. It's got to be well grounded.

A final comment on the business case for a visitor centre, by Ian Jackson, the closest neighbour to The Sill visitor centre:

> This place will be as successful as people choose to make it. That's a platform. It's what goes on in it now that will make it successful, not the building. The building will contribute. Sorry, I don't mean to demean architecture, or construction, or engineers, but it really is. They've put the building there. Now what shall we do with it?

Bringing all of this together, we are now able to say, first, that since we are able to define a coherent set of statements about what a visitor centre is for and that no other building type (especially museums) seems to fulfill this particular combination of purposes, it is certainly *possible* that visitor centres might be a new and emerging building type. Second, having amassed a sample of 43 visitor centres, we can be confident that this is a sufficient number, statistically, to seek commonalities between them. Third, in order to answer the question of whether these really do constitute a new building type, we now need to look for formal, spatial and functional similarities between them (the formal, spatial and functional analyses will be presented in Chapter 4: The Archetypal Visitor Centre) and if these are found, we may then conclude that a new building type has come into existence.

Figure 1.6 The Titan Crane visitor centre: stimulating new visits

2.
Place, Landscape and the Visitor Centre

This chapter will focus, in particular, on the key relationship between place and landscape that is at the very heart of the visitor centre. As Jacob Bronowski says at the beginning of his seminal British television series, *The Ascent of Man*, 'Man[1] is a singular creature. He has a set of gifts, which make him unique among the animals: so that, unlike them, he is not a figure in the landscape – he is a shaper of the landscape'. One reason, for me, as to why the visitor centre is such a fascinating building type is that, for the most part, it sits between a person and the surrounding landscape mediating, and potentially reinforcing, the relationship between the two. The visitor centre is equally dependent upon these two poles: the landscape, or townscape in which it is set and the people who come to visit it. You could argue that this is true, to a greater or lesser degree, for all buildings but for the visitor centre it seems to be particularly apposite. To get this balance right – the relationship between people and landscape or between people and place – appears one of the defining characteristics of a visitor centre (see the previous chapter for its typical functions). It is for this reason that the next two chapters are devoted, in turn, first to landscape and place (Chapter 2) and then to the visitor (Chapter 3).

Introduction to Place and Landscape

Place is a concept that has long been of interest to a diverse range of academic disciplines from architecture and planning to human geography, and from psychology to sociology (and various combinations on the inter-disciplinary fringes of these such as environmental psychology, psycho-geography and urban sociology etc.). Equally, its antonym, 'placelessness' (the state of being devoid of place) has also been the focus of significant academic scrutiny since, as is often the case, it has proved far easier to define and study the absence of place rather than to wrestle with the rather knotty problem of place itself.

What is place, at its most simple and straightforward definition? If space is the empty container, bounded, defined and fixed, but ultimately 'neutral', then a space may become a place if it is further imbued with personal meaning: memories, associations, experiences and reflections. Another, shorthand way of thinking of this is that space is the geometric and the mathematical (quantitative) and place is the personal and emotional (qualitative). All places must also be spaces (i.e. have a spatial definition), but not all spaces will become elevated to the status of place.

If we move on to considering place, not in isolation, but with reference to landscape (since this is the focus of the chapter), then 'landscape' is the more common term, as most people are already aware of the aesthetic potential of certain landscapes (and the *landscape painting*, for example, is a strong part of our cultural heritage), whereas 'place' is the more unusual term, tending to be found in academic texts rather than in mainstream conversation. It could be suggested that the key distinction between place and landscape is that a place tends to be somewhere that we inhabit or occupy. When 'in a place' we are fully immersed in it: it surrounds us and we are often quite unconscious of it. In contrast to this, a landscape is something that we are typically outside of and are looking at, from specific (even pre-defined) vantage points and, furthermore, it is something of which we are often directly aware. The majority of the visitor centres in this book contain both of these experiences in abundance. They are places in which we can meaningfully 'be' and they are located in landscapes that we can admire from afar. It is therefore appropriate that we consider how the ideas of place and landscape may inform the design of the visitor centre.

Cresswell, in his short introduction to place, suggests that there are five key factors that define a place, namely that it should have a fixed position in the world, that it is a setting for social interactions, that it should be meaningful for us, i.e. we have some sort of emotional attachment or response to it (these first three criteria were adapted by Cresswell from John Agnew's 1987 work), that it should also be a definable space and that it should not be a landscape, i.e. somewhere to be viewed rather than inhabited ('People don't live in landscapes they look at them' (Cresswell 2004, p. 11)). If we briefly consider these definitions with respect to visitor centres, they are unarguably in a fixed location in the world and their constituent spaces are physically defined and bounded. They are undoubtedly settings for social interactions and they often affect us emotionally (sometimes even profoundly – consider the visitor centres located at battle sites, Bannockburn and Culloden, for the clearest examples of this; Bannockburn was the site of Robert the Bruce's victory over the English in 1314, and Culloden marks the final battle of the Jacobite uprising in 1746). With respect to landscapes, the situation becomes less clear and more complex. Many visitor centres in this book are set in some of the most beautiful,

rural landscapes in the United Kingdom: The Sill visitor centre near Hadrian's Wall, Stonehenge on Salisbury Plain and the Giant's Causeway on the northern coast of Northern Ireland to name the most spectacular examples. Conversely, others are located in city centres (the Richard III visitor centre in Leicester – indeed, part of it occupying a couple of parking bays in a nondescript, municipal car park; the Cutty Sark visitor centre in historic Greenwich and the Beefeater Gin Distillery visitor centre in residential Kennington, London. These landscapes (or cityscapes) are also, clearly, an important part of the setting for these visitor centres, but are perhaps not as important for the urban visitor centres as for the rural ones.

A slightly different view is provided by David Seamon, who suggests that it is useful to consider that place-related concepts tend to be 'larger than the sum of [their] parts' and that if we attempt to operationalise it too much we risk eliminating the 'phenomenological essence of place' that lies at the heart of it (Seamon, 1987, p. 20). By phenomenological essence he means what it is that can be directly experienced by someone in that location. For Seamon this test of *direct experience* seems to outweigh many of Cresswell's more pragmatic criteria (the fixed location, definable space, social setting definitions). I would tend to agree with Seamon, that of all Cresswell's key points, it is the meaningfulness (related to Seamon's 'phenomenological essence') that is of greatest import.

Much of our current discourse on place has origins in Edward Relph's *Place and Placelessness*, first published in 1976. In his preface to the most recent, reprinted edition of the book, he suggests that the binary distinction between place and placelessness, namely that a location will fall neatly into one of these two types, is a fallacy and that in fact the majority of locations tend to fall somewhere on a continuum between these two extremes. He even suggests that there might be problems associated at either extreme of the spectrum. At the most extreme degree of 'placefullness', there is a danger of being too inwardly focused, with an excessive narrowness of interests, or parochialism (homes and small villages/communities are two examples of exceedingly

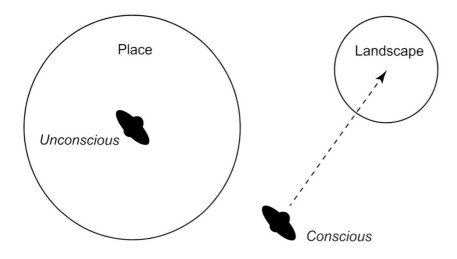

Figure 2.1 **The relationship between a person and place (left) vs a person and landscape (right)**

'placefull' environments). At the other end of the spectrum, locations that are truly 'placeless' (airports, motorway service stations and shopping centres are usually the examples given: they could be, and are, located anywhere) can easily run the risk of a 'surfeit of sameness' (Relph, 2008, pp. iv–v). He goes on to explain that, 'Everywhere has manifestations of both distinctiveness and standardisation … there are exceptional settings in which place is dominant and placelessness is subservient' (ibid.). Interestingly enough, the examples that Relph gives for such 'exceptional settings' are the Acropolis in Athens and Tintern Abbey in Monmouthshire, Wales. This is particularly interesting and relevant for this book, as I would like to suggest that many visitor centres featured in this book are located in precisely the kinds of *exceptional settings* that Relph suggests are one of the very few place-dominant locations. Again, consider Stonehenge, the Giant's Causeway and Hadrian's Wall – clearly these would stand alongside the Acropolis as exceptional settings.

This therefore begs the very real question of what kinds of buildings should be designed for

place-rich, exceptional settings? The initial, knee-jerk, and somewhat glib response is clearly that we need exceptional architecture. (And this is also, probably, why the clients of many potential visitor centres have gone to great lengths, often holding international competitions, to find exactly the right architect capable of producing such an exceptional building). Stuart Evans, Head of Corporate Services at the Northumberland National Park Authority, one of the clients for The Sill visitor centre, echoed this sentiment, when he said, 'I think you start from saying you want something that's going to be exceptional, but you [also] want something that reflects the nature of what makes that exceptional'. Ivor Crowther of the Heritage Lottery Fund says something similar:

How can we marry it into the landscape without putting a, kind of, blot on the landscape? I've seen buildings that are totally out of context within the landscape. You think 'What was the thought at that point?' Was it to create an exceptional building or was it to actually create something special within a special place? If you get that balance right – creating something special in a special place – then it gels well and it's accepted.

It is interesting that both the funder and the client of The Sill visitor centre emphasise that it is not enough just to try and design an exceptional building without it also being appropriate to the context. I would agree yet go even further by suggesting that only seeking to construct an exceptional building (an iconic building would be another way of phrasing this) can create a tension between the building and the attraction or 'resource', whereby each potentially competes with the other for attention. We clearly do not want to have the attention drawn away from the main visitor attraction by a building that is trying to set itself up as being more dominant than the main attraction, namely the very reason that the visitors are drawn to the site in the first place.

The next, predictable, response to the above statement is that what is surely needed, therefore, is effectively an *invisible* building, one that is so *self-effacing* that it blends into the natural landscape. Although he was talking about a somewhat different subject, the idea of the subservient or deferential building is very reminiscent of a quote by the artist Ronald Woodall. Here, he describes the pleasurable, visual aesthetics of ruined, vernacular buildings:

A building must be one with the land and have surrendered to the elements. It must not be an intruder on the landscape, but rather it must be part of the landscape. It must have fused with the earth, capitulated to the wind, bent and bowed with the snows and camouflaged itself in a coating of age. (Woodall, 1976)

This idea of a building being at one with its setting would surely be the ultimate goal of the self-effacing approach to designing visitor centres, whereby site, landscape and context are prioritised above other needs and constraints.

Among the visitor centres featured in, and researched for this book there are certainly examples of visitor centres that make what can be

considered self-effacing gestures, for example, by being partially sunk into the ground, as are parts of the Yorkshire Sculpture Park or Giant's Causeway visitor centres, or through their use of vernacular materials and architectural styles such as is found in Welney or Brockholes visitor centres, or even by their sensitive reuse of existing buildings, as in the case of Whitby Abbey and Wycoller Aisled Barn visitor centres (see Figure 2.2). The client for The Sill visitor centre, Stuart Evans, describes the way in which The Sill tries to blend in with the landscape: 'I think keeping the rough edges, respecting the formation of the rock, respecting how it could blend into the landscape and look like the landscape was the key thing. I think it tells the story well, that you've got a building that's trying to reflect the landscape in how it's shaped and the materials that it uses'.

However, I would like to suggest that there is an equal risk in trying to produce a self-effacing, almost invisible building. Although it might meet all the functional needs and requirements of its visitors, it is possible that it might do so in such a perfunctory manner that it may not be as joyful or inspiring as architecture should surely be. In being subservient to the setting, the architect is introducing just the kind of 'surfeit of sameness' into the building that Relph associates with the convenience-architecture of the non-place. From an architect's perspective, either of these two approaches (the 'iconic' or 'invisible' buildings) appears highly principled: if pursuing the first approach, the architect will believe that they are merely trying to fulfil the client's wish to design an 'exceptional' building to enhance their site or attraction and for the second approach they are nobly repressing their own ego in honour of the landscape.

Alison Thornton-Sykes, Project Architect for The Sill visitor centre, also rejects the idea that a building designed for an exceptional setting should be invisible:

[Should the visitor centre be] self-effacing? I think it's a bold landscape, isn't it? So, I think you have to be unapologetic and bold in it, and there is a time and a place for the softer [approach] – and

I think that's why we've tried to orientate the building so that on the southern side, which is a softer, more undulating landscape, the building has its curves and a softness to it. But then, when you return on the building, and you rise up to that projection, out into that outcrop, which is incredibly hard, angular, stark and austere, you want to stand up to it, in respect. And also to give the visitor that exhilaration, that experience of feeling, 'Wow, I'm up here. I'm elevated, and I'm out in that landscape. Look what I can go off and explore next.' So, I think the building has to respect what's around it, but respond to it, I think, and speak back to it.

She goes on to describe the potential for tension between the building and the landscape, and how they ensured they did not fall into this trap.

[In order not to compete with the landscape] we did a landscape visual impact assessment as part of the process, as well, which [included] lots of important studies and views from key vantage points, to make sure that, when you're up on Hadrian's Wall, looking back, it doesn't dominate the landscape, and it's not overpowering, and it's only glimpsed from certain viewpoints.

Is there, as Alison Thornton-Sykes' observation suggests, a third way? An approach to architectural design that is different again to competing with or surrendering to the setting? (And there are visitor centres that are guilty, to a greater or lesser degree, of either of these approaches). The third way is what might be termed designing a *synergistic building*. This is by far the hardest to achieve and only a selection of the visitor centres researched for this book manage the degree of balance and control required to achieve this (see Figure 2.7). To design a synergistic building, both the building and the setting serve to heighten the visitor's experience of the other, see Figure 2.3. How might these be achieved?

Figure 2.2 The sensitive reuse of existing buildings: Whitby Abbey (left) and Wycoller Aisled Barn (right) visitor centres

For a synergistic building, both the visitor centre and the building must be adding something to the other, and this relationship must be reciprocal. I would like to suggest that what it is that the architecture contributes to the exceptional setting is a way of enhancing the already present, sense of place experienced by its visitors. In return, what the 'exceptional setting' is giving to the architecture is a sort of vicarious authenticity, in other words, the building feels more 'authentic' by association with the exceptional setting. In the remainder of this chapter, I will expand upon both halves of this synergistic relationship.

The Enhancing of Place

In the previous chapter, I suggested that one of the ways in which a visitor centre can be considered to be distinct from a museum is that a visitor centre is about *having an experience* rather than being explicitly about *acquiring knowledge*. Can a 'synergistic' building help a visitor to have such an experience? (And can it do this better than an 'iconic' or an 'invisible' building?). A visitor centre can help to heighten the experience of an attraction, setting or resource in a number of different ways: the framing of views of settings (Figure 2.4 shows some examples of how visitor centres can be used to frame the setting); the careful sequencing and pacing of the visit/route/path; narrative control over the building; the building's orientation/placement on site and finally, to be a place in its own right (as distinct from the setting) while still ensuring a deep resonance between the building's sense of place and the place identity of the setting. It is this latter approach (the relationship between the experience of place in the building and the sense of place of the site) to enhancing people's sense of place that I will expand upon in the next section, as it is both the most important and the least intuitive of the approaches.

In David Seamon's paper on the design of the Olana visitor centre, Hudson, New York (the home of the American landscape painter, Frederic Church, 1826–1900), he explains how the original vision for

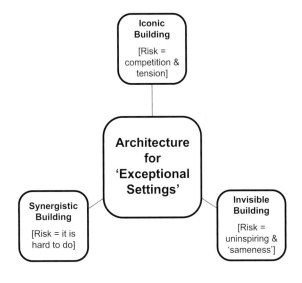

Figure 2.3 Three different approaches to architecture for exceptional settings

the (as yet unbuilt) Olana visitor centre was that the building should evoke some of the parallel experiences and meanings of the house and estate itself, for example, the significance of view, both literally and spiritually (Church was a devoted Christian believing in Manifest Destiny[2] (Seamon, 1992)). This is one theory of how a sense of place, of the setting or the resource, may be heightened, namely by reflecting back some aspect of the original setting, through the design of the building. The analogy here is the *visitor centre as a mirror*. But mirrors reflect what is, at best, a perfect copy of the original or, at worst, a poor reproduction of it. The reflection must always be lesser or equivalent to the original. Therefore, a building might attempt to refashion the same sense of place, but no more.

For this reason, there is a slightly different analogy, which I would like to use in this chapter. This

is the idea of the *visitor centre as a lens*, to the extent that it not only reflects back some aspect of the setting but also *focuses* the visitors' sense of 'place' in the same way that a lens can be used to focus light to a point. This bears some similarities to ideas that Edward Casey outlined in his book, *Getting Back into Place*, where he describes how a building can be considered a *focus locorum* (a focuser of place), or indeed a *locus locorum*, a 'place for places', but does not expand on how this might be realised in practice (Casey, 1993, p. 32). He does, however, go on to suggest that, 'A building condenses a culture in one place' (ibid., p. 32) so just as a synergistic building is able to focus attention away from itself by curating and controlling views to the landscape from inside

the building (to use but one architectural device), so it must also strive to be a 'place' in its own right, by focusing or 'condensing' (after Casey) the cultural meaning of the attraction. See Figure 2.5 for a diagram showing analogies of the visitor centre as mirror and as lens.

This idea of the building as a lens that serves to focus the attention of visitors was an analogy that many of the stakeholder interviewees for The Sill visitor centre were in agreement with. Ivor Crowther of the Heritage Lottery Fund stated,

> It does focus people's attention. If they have a focal point to go towards, then the likelihood of them understanding that place and the

Figure 2.4 Framed views: Woodhorn Museum and Northumberland Archives (top); Alnwick Gardens (above); Virginia Water (right)

surrounding landscape of the national park is far, far greater. I think it's a combination [of] what is actually happening in the building with the exhibitions and the education that [means] people will focus on that as a key gateway to the rest of the park.

Stuart Evans, of the Northumberland National Park Authority, expanded upon this idea of the lens:

It's that lens through which people can see [the site], yes. If we go back, visitor centres used to give people lots of information. We're now trying to point people in the way of an experience. For people who've come before, they can go out better equipped to do something else. For those that don't like journeying, we've put [the visitor centre] in a place where you just step outside and, within ten minutes, you can walk to the Tree of the Year, i.e. to the Sycamore Gap, something that's quite cognisant to most people. Yes, the 'lens' is a good way [of thinking about it] … it's not an end in itself; it's a means to equip people to then go out and either discover things or do more.

Alison Thornton-Sykes was very much in agreement with this concept. She commented,

I think [focusing people's attention] is one of the main jobs of a visitor centre. That's exactly what it needs to do, particularly if you are potentially visiting only once. It needs to get that message across in quite a relatively short space of time, doesn't it? You need to have that element of excitement, surprise, 'wow' factor, that really grabs people's attention, and magnifies these amazing characteristics that are out there in the landscape to really engage people.

And finally, the nearest neighbour to The Sill visitor centre, Ian Jackson, drew a contrast with other ways in which a sense of place might be explicitly reinforced, if not achieved subtly through the building-as-lens: 'I think it's quite reasonable to reinforce place – I would hope they [the architects] would – as

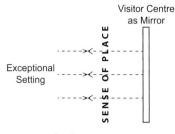

Visitor Centre as Mirror

After Seamon, 1992

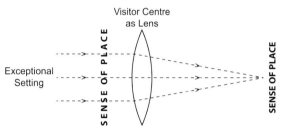

Visitor Centre as Lens

(After Casey, 1993) & Conroy Dalton, 2017

Figure 2.5 The visitor centre 'as mirror' (after Seamon, 1992) and 'as lens' analogies (after Casey, 1993; Conroy Dalton, 2017)

a device, rather than have everything as a series of audio-visuals or exhibits in a museum. It's in the subconscious, isn't it? We walk through it'.

If we return to the beginning of this section, to the list of ways in which, it is suggested, this focusing of place might be realised, the last point was *to be a place in its own right* (as distinct from the setting) while ensuring a deep resonance between the building's sense of place and the place identity of the setting. It is clear that since the building is serving as a focus of 'place' then it must also be a place itself (Casey's *locus locorum*) – as something distinct and separate from the attraction or the setting (and it is for this reason that bland and invisible architecture will not serve this purpose) – but that the sense of place of the architecture must resonate with the place identity of the setting, and this is how the setting can add something to the architecture. The very fact that the site *already has* a strong sense of place can give guidance to the architect on how the sense of place may then be articulated in the building. Different aspects of the site may indicate the way in which the sense of place of the setting is reflected by the visitor centre. This quality can be different for each visitor centre (if the setting is ruinous, Fountains Abbey for example, it might not make sense or be appropriate for the visitor centre to reflect the ruined aspect of the abbey – indeed, 'faked' ruins would feel inauthentic). Conversely, when trying to focus people's sense of place, architects might try to identify aspects of the site that can be shared by both the setting and the visitor centre. Whichever approach is taken, however, there should nevertheless be a strong connection between the visitor centre building and the site.

Casey later suggests:

What is paramount in a culturally specified place ... is the experience of *being* in that place and, more particularly, *becoming part of the place*. The time of cultural implacement (and the time experienced *in* that implacement) is that which informs a place in concert with other human beings, through one's bodily agency, within the embrace of a landscape. (ibid., p. 33)

What is interesting about this quote is that Casey is raising the difference between already feeling in place (a state) and 'becoming part of the place' (a process) with reference to the wider landscape and this distinction is clearly highly relevant to visitor centres. It is important that the building should provide the visitor with a sense of place. But given that place is usually associated with 'place attachment', which is the combination of emotions, meanings and significance imbued in a location through the everyday lived experience of being in it (and usually for an extended period of time: people's strong attachment to their home is the typical example given), then how can a building be expected to invoke a sense of place – the creation of

a meaningful, affective experience – for a visitor who is most likely *a first time visitor*,[3] i.e., exactly those individuals without such a lived experience of place?

I would like to suggest that it is certainly possible for people to identify with a place or find a place meaningful, even as a first time visitor, since our experience of a place frequently starts long before we actually visit it. Take Stonehenge as an example. How many visitors going to visit Stonehenge for the first time, are not already acquainted with it in some manner? They may have studied it at school, read factual books (or novels[4]) about it or set in it, seen documentaries on the archaeology or science or astronomy of it, watched films set there,[5] heard the annual news stories about the gatherings of modern druids to celebrate the summer solstice, had family members or friends who have already visited it, etc. Even the first-time visitor arrives not without a prior, 'at-a-distance' encounter (perhaps this might be termed 'tele-experience' or 'tele-place') with the site. In fact, the most immediate response of many first-time visitors to the Stonehenge monument is that the stone circle appears much smaller than imagined; so familiar do they 'feel' with the site, that the physical reality of the sizes of the stones may come as a genuine surprise. Therefore, in the case of Stonehenge, it is clearly wrong to say that we do not already have some kind of a 'lived-experience' of the site. But where such at-a-distance experiences are formed, they are frequently examples of the cultural, vicarious, lived-experiences, as described above.

Relph suggests that with our increasingly mobile and interconnected (i.e. the world wide web) everyday experiences, the extent of aspatial and non-local experiences has 'broken down barriers of that rooted sense of place' (Relph, 2008 Preface, pp. iv–v). The idea that we can only feel a meaningful connection with a place with which we are intimately familiar is no longer as relevant (if it ever were). Relph explains further:

Increased travel and mobility, combined with the electronic intercommunications that are now taken for granted, have broken down the barriers of that rooted sense of place. The narrow but deep experience that once was normal has given way to briefer experiences of many different places. This is a trade-off. It constitutes a loss because deeply focused and meaningful experience has been replaced by the outsideness of relatively fleeting and touristic encounters ... A corollary is that a strong sense of place is not necessarily related with length of time lived somewhere. It is possible for somebody to have little affection for somewhere they have lived in drudgery for decades, or, conversely, to develop deep connections with somewhere that they have known only for a few days. (ibid.)

It should be noted that Relph, in the first edition of *Place and Placelessness*, was somewhat critical of the heritage industry, accusing it of the 'Disneyfication' of historic environments. But in the more recent edition of his book, he has moderated that opinion, just as the heritage industry has matured over the intervening decades, and he suggests that the heritage industry has a very important role to play in preserving 'exceptional settings' and ensuring that they have a relevant future (ibid.). This, in turn, echoes the views of Casey (1993, p. 33) who says, of culturally significant settings:

> The cultural dimension of place – along with affiliated historical, social and political aspects and avatars – adds something quite new to the earlier analysis [of place], something we had not yet encountered in our reflections on the logic and experience of place. This dimension contributes to the felt density of a particular place, the sense that it has something lasting in it.

It is clearly this concept of the perceived 'density'[6] of place combined with a sense of the longevity of a setting that many culturally important settings – exceptional settings – have, which will ensure, as Relph says, that such settings will continue to feel relevant to us and will have an important future. This section of the chapter concludes by suggesting that this future is one that visitor centres (if designed in a 'synergistic' rather than an 'iconic' or 'invisible' way) will play their part in safeguarding. But we need now to explore the other side of the

synergistic relationship between the visitor centre and its setting: if the visitor centre helps focus our sense of place, what does the setting, the landscape, do for the visitor centre?

Vicarious Authenticity

It was suggested earlier in this chapter that the way in which a location or setting can enhance a visitor centre is to give it something I am calling 'vicarious authenticity'. So how does an exceptional setting serve to make architecture feel more 'authentic' by association? And what exactly do we mean by authenticity? In any discussion of heritage or cultural tourism, the word 'authenticity' will very soon arise and is a term that engenders some debate in the heritage and tourism literature. Without diving deep into this debate, for the sake of this book, we can say simply that authenticity is clearly the opposite of deliberate deception or 'fakery', and so is surely about, in some manner, enabling the visitor to access the true essence of a 'real' place.

The stakeholders of The Sill visitor centre had clear views on the concept of authenticity. Stuart Evans, Head of Corporate Services at the Northumberland National Park Authority, was quick to point out that, 'Authenticity, I think, is something that people respect and something to value as a visitor'. He goes on to state, later in the interview, 'We see authenticity of the landscape as something that we have to do to tell the story, but we think that we're doing it in a context whereby people are [already] looking for that authenticity in their "leisure time"'. He concludes his thoughts on the authenticity of visitor centres by observing, 'In terms of the authenticity, we think we're getting it right and this needs to be not just about the design of the building but authenticity should also influence the choice of food sold and the types of goods sold at The Sill'.

If we return to the earlier statement that to design buildings for exceptional settings, the ideal approach is the 'synergistic building' in which the building helps to focus the visitors' sense of place and that the building is further enhanced by a sense of 'vicarious' authenticity, it can be suggested that this is less about the authenticity of the attraction or resource itself (although any visitor centre would undoubtedly wish to ensure this as well), and more about whether they experience the visitor centre as an authentic building that is appropriate to its setting.

In architecture, as well as in tourism, authenticity (or 'honesty') is by no means an unfamiliar term: the phrase 'honest materials', meaning that a material's physical properties should dictate how it is used, or 'structural honesty', meaning that structural elements should do what they appear to be doing and not be merely decorative (for example, a decorative arch that is not load-bearing), are philosophies that are very familiar to architects. However, in 'Reality and authenticity in the experience economy', Michael Benedikt describes how historically architecture has also had 'many long flirtations with illusion and artifice. Poised between nature and culture, architecture, even at its most fanciful, has always shown two faces at once, the real and the unreal' (Benedikt, 2001). He goes on to suggest that since we have reached the technological stage where, with the help of computers, just about anything that can be imagined by an architect can be built, he suggests that many architects have responded to this by seeking an 'absolute "honesty" of construction' (ibid.). Benedikt suggests that many architects are seeking true authenticity, or 'the authority that comes from being real without trying.' He then goes on to make the following, interesting statement:

> And there's the rub. The moment one tries to be real, tries to be authentic, and the trying is detected, the bubble bursts and inauthenticity spills out. But all is not lost; there is some middle ground. The best actors can make us forget they're acting … Can architects – or, rather, their buildings – do the same? … The authenticity of an architecture that takes as its goal the embodiment of quiet realness should be possible to achieve. (ibid., 2001)

So if this search for true authenticity in building is indeed the goal of many architects, how

can being 'real without trying' or creating 'the embodiment of quiet realness' be achieved, to use Benedikt's phrase? In 'The Quest for Authenticity and the Replication of Environmental Meaning' (Dovey, 1985), Kim Dovey makes a slightly different suggestion, namely that authenticity is about the relationship or 'connectedness' between a person and their environment. He states that, 'Authenticity is a condition of integrity in person-environment relationships. This connectedness is not a perceptual phenomenon; its deeper significance lies not in its connection of appearance to reality, but in its connection of people to their world. Authenticity is, then, a way of being-in-the-world' (ibid., p. 47). Dovey suggests three relationships between people's everyday experiences and the environment, which together form the different components of authenticity: all of which are relevant for the context of the visitor centre and the question of how to design an authentic architectural building. What is most interesting about Dovey's three relationships is that they differ temporally: one is about looking back in time, the second is firmly rooted in the present and the third looks forward to the future.

The first of these, which is the one that looks back in time, is about the origin of a material or object. We are very familiar with the idea of an object having an undisputed origin, and we even have a word for this, which is its *provenance* or a record of ownership of an object stretching back in time to its origin. But Dovey also uses this concept of having an undisputed origin to refer also to the materiality of a building or building components. For him, the undisputed origin of a material is about the process by which it was made. A piece of timber has the properties that it has (and this is how it differs from other wood-derived products such as MDF or particle board) because of the way in which a tree grows and is it this process of organic growth that gives wood its particular properties of strength and appearance (and why MDF can never be mistaken for wood). Cast iron has very different properties and appearance to wrought iron, even though they both contain iron and this is because of the very different methods used in their production. Cast iron trying to look as if it has been worked in a blacksmith's forge is therefore unauthentic. Dovey is simply saying is that an object can only be authentic if its history is authentic (and hasn't, for example, been given a fake patina of ageing) and that a material can only be authentic if it has been produced in a manner consistent with how that material is typically produced or manufactured.

The second of Dovey's components of authenticity is the relationship between the outward appearance of something and its materiality or substance (or its 'genuineness', to use Dovey's term). This is similar to the concept of honesty in materials in architecture, as mentioned previously. If something looks like a wooden beam, it should be a wooden beam and not a reproduction beam cast from resin. This relationship between person and environment is embedded in the present as it is all about a person's direct experience of the world.

The third and final relationship, according to Dovey, connecting our perception of an environment and its reality is the relationship between an object's future performance and our expectations of it (or its 'reliability or trustworthiness'). If a window, therefore, looks as if it *could* be opened, then it must be able to be opened – our expectations of its function should be met. Therefore, according to Dovey, it is not enough to say that something is merely 'authentic', rather it should have all of these three properties, it should have undisputed origins, *be* on the inside as it *appears to be* on the outside and function in the way we would expect it to do. If these three relationships are met, then somewhere, or something (even a visitor centre) will feel authentic and will potentially feel 'real without trying'.

One aspect of visiting and researching the visitor centres in this book that has been conspicuous, is the extent to which architects and clients have striven to select local materials: stones from local quarries, trees felled on the estate in which the visitor centre is located and planting that is representative of the local flora. Stuart Evans of The Northumbria National Park described how important the use of local materials and the inclusion of local flora were to the design of The Sill visitor centre:

I think the fact that 80 per cent of the materials on the outside [of the building] are of the area allows you to tell a good story. I think the way that it's designed into the landscape with deliberate rough edges on the North and a warmer Southern face … I think that plays into it and tells people about it. I think the unique selling point we have is the Whin Sill grass roof, [in] which [we are] putting in something like 80,000 to 100,000 plants and plugs (but all 80 to 88 types of plants you would expect to find in Northumberland) so there is something about that that just makes it ring [with people].

Alison Thornton-Sykes, also described the importance of using local materials to achieve authenticity:

If the building responds to the site and its setting, so that there's an experience to be had for the visitor, and they become really engaged with the building, and with its wider setting, [then] I think it can be done on a material level: using local sandstone and whinstone to express the geological strata that would happen in Northumberland, but also that really links the building back to its earth, to its site, combined with very warm, natural materials like timber, and the planting and the green roofs, are bringing in that natural world. So, you're creating a whole palette of very welcoming, warm materials that resonate with that site, so that people get an immediate sense of what the site is about. I think you may only visit it once, but you have a good feel and a strong idea of what the site is about.

And, Stuart Evans again,

The building: local sandstone cut and finished in nearby Haltwhistle … We've tried to keep it as irregular as possible (noting that the doors are still rectangle, as are the windows, and there's a damp-proof course that's horizontal) … so there was a lot of effort just to get that right – get the right stone and get the right craftspeople working on it as well.

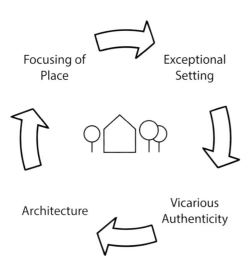

Figure 2.6 The synergistic building: a synergistic relationship between architecture and the exceptional setting

And Ivor Crowther, of the Heritage Lottery Fund, also stressed the importance of using local materials in order to be authentic:

> I think [the visual appearance of visitor centres is about] using a variety of materials to understand its concept of the landscape. I think that's why you've got a lot of timber on this building, because there's a lot of woodland there. You've got the Whin Sill and the gabions that are packed with the Whin Sill [stone], so it gives a relation to the geology.

It is clear that, as long as the building strives to be authentic (and not comply with a 'Disneyesque' architecture of explicit fakery), to be honest with materials, structures and forms, then the 'vicarious authenticity' that the building derives from its setting achieves what Benedikt is talking about, *to be real without trying*, and also what Dovey describes

about the relationship between what we experience of the world and its reality matching. The exceptional setting bestows on the building an additional impetus, and an authority, to be real. And, from the perspective of the visitors, there is a prior expectation that the visitor centre (as well as the attraction) will be authentic, and each in their own way. It is this additional drive to be authentic, and the public's expectation of authenticity, that I am terming 'vicarious authenticity'. The visitor centre does not necessarily have to be authentic in its own right, but because it is inextricably linked to the attraction or resource, then there are greater expectations from the visitors that it should be. See Figure 2.6 for a diagram explaining how this contributes to the synergistic relationship between visitor centre and landscape.

Returning to the definition of a synergistic building, the corollary is that each component (the building and the setting) gives something to the other. The landscape gives to the building (vicarious authenticity) and the building provides something in return to the landscape (a focusing of place) so that each part (the building and the landscape) is more than it would be by itself. This is why it is a synergistic relationship: the overall result (if done well) is clearly more than the sum of the parts: each part is enhanced by the other.

In order to test these measures for the subset of 20 buildings (the exemplar case studies presented in the second part of the book) each visitor centre was evaluated to determine where it lay on this tripartite iconicity/invisibility/synergy measure. To evaluate them, an analytic hierarchy process (AHP) was used in which each possible pair of buildings was compared. For example, when evaluating a pairing of The Mary Rose visitor centre and the Stonehenge visitor centre, and with respect to their relative amounts of 'iconicism', a judgement was made on which of the two buildings was the more 'iconic' and by how much (on a given scale). This was then repeated for every possible set of building-pairs and for all three of the measures. Each visitor centre then received a value for how iconic it was, how invisible and how synergistic.[7] These values were plotted on a triangular-graph containing three axes.

The closer to a corner-point of the triangle (labelled with the three different building properties) a visitor centre was located, the more of that attribute it was deemed to have, see Figure 2.7.

From this figure we can see that the most iconic building in the subset of twenty buildings is the Stonehenge visitor centre; the most invisible building is the Chedworth Roman Villa visitor centre; and the most synergistic building is the Wycoller Aisled Barn visitor centre. It is also interesting to see where buildings lie on the mid-points between two terms. For example, Welney Wetland visitor centre is almost equally synergistic and iconic (but far from being invisible) and Abbotsford visitor centre scores highly on both the 'invisibility' and 'synergy' criteria but is not very iconic. Some visitor centres score

equally as well on all three aspects, and are therefore located towards the centre of the diagram: in this case, these very 'balanced' visitor centres are the Giant's Causeway and Alnwick Gardens visitor centres.

This chapter has focused primarily on the relationship between the visitor centre and its setting, the landscape and the strong sense of place evoked by many of these sites. However, the other, equally important component in the design of visitor centres are the visitors themselves. As stated at the beginning of this chapter, the visitor centre sits between the visitor and the landscape mediating between the two and its existence is equally dependent upon both. In the next chapter we will, therefore, turn to the role of the visitor.

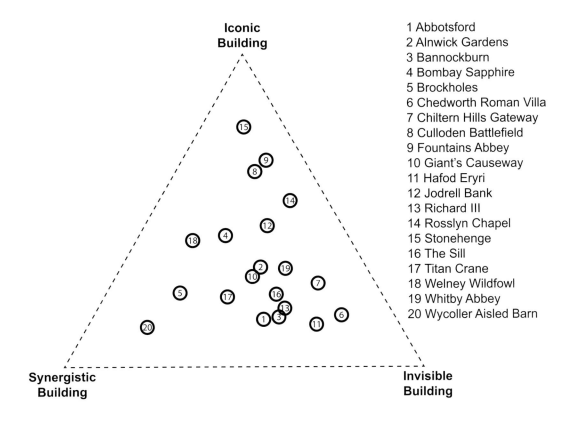

1 Abbotsford
2 Alnwick Gardens
3 Bannockburn
4 Bombay Sapphire
5 Brockholes
6 Chedworth Roman Villa
7 Chiltern Hills Gateway
8 Culloden Battlefield
9 Fountains Abbey
10 Giant's Causeway
11 Hafod Eryri
12 Jodrell Bank
13 Richard III
14 Rosslyn Chapel
15 Stonehenge
16 The Sill
17 Titan Crane
18 Welney Wildfowl
19 Whitby Abbey
20 Wycoller Aisled Barn

Figure 2.7 The relative degrees to which 20 visitor centres are iconic, synergistic and invisible

3.
The Visitor

In many respects visitors are the most important subjects in a book on the architecture of visitor centres, since without them, the visitor centre would be without purpose: illogical and meaningless. This chapter will begin by considering the visitor: the history of the visitor; who they are; why do they visit visitor centres and what are they looking for? The second part of the chapter will discuss how the architect designs for the visitor and seeks to take their needs into account.

The Visitor in History

Visiting places of historical, cultural or natural interest is hardly a new phenomenon. The first visitor centre that we are aware of, or that could possibly be honoured with this title, was located at Stonehenge in the mid-eighteenth century. This period marked the beginning of a British interest in making excursions to visit notable sites around the UK (Ousby, 2002) and the visitor centre at Stonehenge was merely a response to this new and extremely fashionable pastime; it consisted of a hut, located next to one of the fallen, inner sarsen stones, from which drinks were sold, with an excavated pit below the stone used to provide cool storage. The enterprising 'owner' of the hut, one Gaffer Hunt of nearby Amesbury, would also proffer his services as guide to the site (in this example, we have here the early equivalent of cafe/storage/exhibition combined with interactive guide).

'One Gaffer Hunt of Ambresbury built a hut against the upright stone of Mars; and attended there daily with liquors, to entertain the traveller, and shew him the stones: his cellar was under the great stone, next the hut' (Smith, 1771, p. 52).

Moving forward in time, in *A History of Holidays 1812–1990*, Bill Cormack suggests that we can trace an increase in the numbers of people taking holidays and making day excursions to sites to an increase in wealth at the beginning of the nineteenth century. This is a very practical explanation for the increase in these activities, but further on in the book, when discussing the sudden popularity of going to the seaside, he observes, 'there was nothing new about going to the seaside. It had *merely become fashionable*' (1998, p. 14, my italics). This comment is quite an interesting one, as we may ask of modern visitor centres, the question: Is there a sense, at this moment in time, that perhaps there is nothing really new about the visitor centre, per se (especially if we can trace the *ur-type* visitor centre back to the mid-1700s at Stonehenge) but rather that there is also the sense that, at the cusp of the twentieth and twenty-first centuries, visitor centres have simply become 'fashionable' in exactly the same way that the seaside resort suddenly became 'fashionable' in the first half of the nineteenth century? (The presumed 'fashionableness' of visitor centres is based on the visitor data in Figure 3.1 and on the number of architectural award-winning visitor centres built since 1990, in Chapter 4, Figure 4.3).

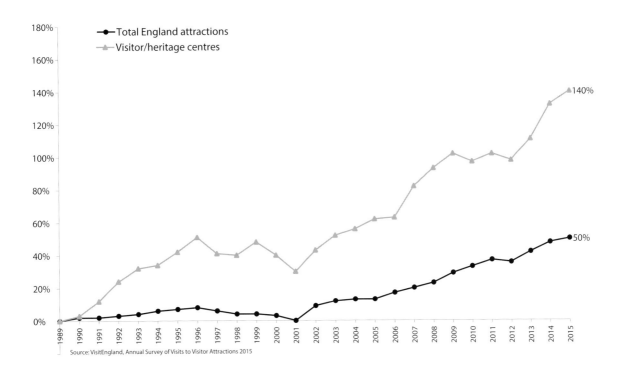

Proportion increase since 1989 of visits to visitor/heritage centres compared to total attractions in England

Source: VisitEngland, Annual Survey of Visits to Visitor Attractions 2015

But how or why does an attraction suddenly become fashionable? In *The Englishman's England* (Ousby, 2002), there is a suggestion that what appeals to people are certain kinds of attraction, primarily nature, literary or historical sites. This was, in Ousby's opinion, the origin of visitor centres. He considers a number of different types of attraction in his book: places connected with writers (Abbotsford visitor centre is an example in this book), country houses (the closest example would be the Alnwick Gardens visitor centre), ancient monuments (Stonehenge visitor centre), medieval ruins (Whitby Abbey visitor centre) and the natural landscape (Giant's Causeway visitor centre) and makes a connection between their rise in popularity and a change in people's 'taste'. 'By taste ... I mean the application of general tendencies of thought and cultural attitude to the act of judging one aspect

of our environment as interesting, beautiful or otherwise worth attention and rejecting others as not. Travel quickly converts these judgments into practical, local and specific terms' (Ousby, 2002, p. 5). Ousby, therefore, directly connects this definition of taste, or the 'the act of judging one aspect of our environment as ... worth attention', with the rise in popularity of a type of attraction. And so, bringing this forward to today, if visitor centres have currently become 'fashionable' (after Cormack), is this perhaps due a recent change or refinement in our collective taste?

If we continue to take the long view on the history of the visitor, we can perhaps arrive at another explanation for the rise in popularity of the visitor centre. Cormack also says in his book that, 'The folk tradition that a holiday was but a day away from work, lasted from medieval times until the

Figure 3.1 Growth of visits to visitor centres since 1989
Source: VisitEngland, Annual Survey of Visits to Visitor Attractions 2015

twentieth century, reinforced by the Bank Holidays Act of 1871' when 'A day off for secular enjoyment was sorely needed ...' (ibid., p. 44). He continues, 'There was one great advantage in going out for the day; it was cheaper than going on holiday. Lots of people have been known to spend their annual holiday in this way, going off each day to somewhere new and returning to their own home at night, thus avoiding the expense of overnight accommodation' (ibid., p. 48). In contrast, we have here a very down-to-earth reason for the growth in day trips: at times of economic hardship, it is simply cheaper to stay at home (and hence the recent appearance of the portmanteau word, 'staycation', meaning 'stay' plus 'vacation'). Certainly, if we consider the VisitEngland figures for the number of visits to visitor centres shown in Figure 3.1, there is undoubtedly a rise in numbers between 2007 and 2008, which coincides with the recent financial crisis.

By continuing to look back into the history of holidaymaking, we can perhaps unpick yet another dimension to the current phenomenon. Cormack describes the growth of day excursions in the twentieth century and how eventually, 'Everyone had become a little blasé about trip and treats, even children and old-age pensioners. What was once an annual event became a weekly possibility but the novelty has disappeared' (ibid., p. 49). And so perhaps this, more than anything else, explains the reason for the recent growth in visitor centres, that, as everyone becomes more blasé about day trips (to use Cormack's phrase) the 'attractions', in response, have had to work much harder to both *attract* and more generally to *please* the visitor. As each one consciously self-improves its offering as a defence against the blasé, so the bar is continuously raised. And so, by looking back over history, we have some indication as to why the visitor centre might be so popular with people today. First, it is merely fashionable (after Cormack) which might be explained due to the changing nature of our taste (Ousby), furthermore it is cheap (Cormack), and its ever-present accessibility and ubiquity has resulted in a frenzy of self-improvement, namely the construction of shiny new visitor centres, as a bulwark against the blasé.

Who is the Modern Visitor?

Without question, there are more people visiting visitor centres (as well as more visitor centres) than in the past. According to VisitEngland (2016), the number of visits to visitor/heritage centres in 2015 were up 2 per cent (and up 8 per cent for 2013/2014) for free visitor centres and up 5 per cent (up 12 per cent for 2013/2014) for fee-paying visitor centres (p. 20) resulting in an average increase of 3 per cent for 2015 and 10 per cent for 2013/2014 (p. 13). (85 visitor centres were surveyed for this data, many of them featured in this book, (p. 4)). A further 15 per cent increase in overseas visitors contributed to this strong trend (p. 24). This also resulted in an increase in gross revenue, which was up by 13 per cent in 2015 (p. 35). As can be seen from the graph in Figure 3.1 (p. 14), this is part of an ongoing trend since 1989: VisitEngland's statistics show that in 2015 the number of people visiting visitor or heritage centres had increased by 140 per cent since 1989 (p. 14).

For an architect designing a visitor centre, or for a client commissioning one, it is important to first understand your visitor profile. Stuart Evans described the process that the client and architect went through, when designing The Sill visitor centre:

We ran a number of discussion groups with different people, and did a lot of market research at the outset to get the concept absolutely right. Then, as we've carried that through the design phase, we've said, 'Right, how do we carry their preferred design through for those people so that it still works for them?' In terms of what we built and what we put in, it was important that we did two things – we consulted the community and visitors on what they wanted to be in there. We held consultation events in the visitor season so we could get their views as well. We also sought views from colleagues, experts, and people who'd run businesses on what they would see working. We went out to schools and to parents' groups from people who don't normally visit the countryside. We [even] went and asked the Chinese Society at Newcastle University, 'What would they want?'

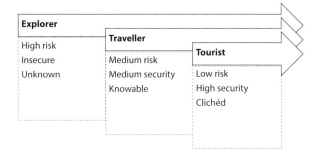

Figure 3.2 Categories of visitor, after Fussell (1982)

In *Abroad*, Fussell (1982) considers three kinds of visitor: the explorer, the traveller and the tourist. I would suggest that rather than see these as three entirely distinct figures, they can be considered to occupy parts of a spectrum, with the traveller placed somewhere in the middle, and the two opposing ends of the spectrum accommodating the explorer (characterised by high risks, lack of security and unknown environments/activities) and the other end, the domain of the tourist (characterised by low risk, ensured security and clichéd rather than unknown activities), see Figure 3.2.

In this spectrum, where do our visitor centre visitors lie? Certainly, the tourist end of the spectrum is fully represented (and a tourist may be international or domestic and includes people making day-trips and visits from home). Many of the visitor centres in this book are there to facilitate the visits to some of the country's main visitor attractions, i.e. Stonehenge and the Giant's Causeway. Others, however, are a little more 'off the beaten track' and could possibly be considered more the domain of the traveller rather than, strictly speaking, the tourist (examples here being the visitor centre at the summit of Snowdon, Wycoller Aisled Barn and the Titan Crane visitor centres).[1] Equally, the accusation of tourism being clichéd or about engaging in clichéd activities, as suggested by Fussell (ibid.), is an aspect of the visit that the architecture of these new visitor centres appears to be striving to dispel (see the section in the previous chapter on authenticity).

Do the majority of people go to visitor centres alone or as part of a group? There is clear evidence (Dickinson et al., 2004) that the majority of visitors to sites form parts of couples or small groups and frequently visit as a family (or multigenerational/extended family groups). So, is it possible to say that there a specific visitor profile: a typical visitor centre patron? Of the sample of visitor centres examined and visited as part of this research, 21 per cent are owned by either English Heritage or the National Trust (or both). We can, therefore, say a little more about this subset of visitor centres. Jon Henly in the *Guardian*, describes the typical National Trust member as 'a mix of earnest – and overwhelmingly white – middle-class parents … and genteel retired couples' (Henley, 2010), and this is a widely-held view. Returning to Dickinson et al., in their survey of the travel methods of visitors to a range of 26 National Trust properties in the South West of England, the authors found that the age of visitors in a group reflected this view, insomuch as 71 per cent of visitors were over the age of 55, and a further 32 per cent were children under 16 years old and therefore were presumably accompanied by parents or grandparents. The least represented group were the 17–24 age group (Dickinson et al., 2004). One of the clients of The Sill visitor centre, the Northumberland National Park Authority, was very aware of the inter-generational character of their potential visitors. As Stuart Evans confirms:

A key design standard we have kept all the way through is 'accessibility'. Increasingly, we are, as a society, living longer. Increasingly, when people go out as families, it isn't just necessarily the two generations. It's generations one and three that might go out. When we look at where we're going to put activity spaces and training areas, we need to design places for granny and grandpa to watch the kids while they're having a cup of coffee.

Of the 8,299 respondents to Dickinson et al.'s survey of National Trust visitors, 15 per cent revealed that they had travelled more than 50 miles to visit the National Trust property that they were visiting when polled/surveyed and that the most common origin for the visit (40 per cent) was their own home, in other words it was a day trip (refer back to Cormack, 1998). Data on how people got to the attraction was only available for five properties in their survey, but the car was the predominant mode of transport in all cases where there were not qualifying reasons against its use (i.e. inaccessible by car). For the vast majority of visitor centres in this book, with only the urban ones as exceptions, the car is by far the easiest way to get there. This does have an implication as to the kinds of people who are able to visit a visitor centre, since according to the National Travel Survey 2014, almost half of households in the lowest income quintile have no access to a car, and those in the wealthiest households (the highest income quintile) tended to travel more than twice as far by car (Department of Transport, 2014). In other words, given that some people are travelling more than 50 miles to visit a National Trust property, these are also likely to be people with a higher than average household income.

In summary, we have been able to build up a profile for a subset of the visitor centres (the National Trust properties) in this book, and can suggest that this profile is probably applicable to the rest of the visitor centres featured. Most visitors travel as a couple or a group and many of these groups are family groups, the average age of a visitor is older compared to other tourist attractions (Dickinson et al., 2004) and many groups include children. The most common way to get to a visitor centre is with a car, which also implies that they are more likely to be from higher, rather than lower, income households. And, finally, that most people are making a day trip and starting out from their own homes.

Why Do People Visit?

In their research on visitor experiences at heritage sites, Masberg and Silverman conducted a phenomenological approach to surveying visitors by focusing, in particular, on their *experiences* and asking them to describe them in detail. These descriptions were subsequently analysed and the authors were able to identify seven distinct themes from these elicited, open-ended responses (Masberg and Silverman, 1996). The authors classified these experiences as being about: activities; companions; site personnel; information; the built environment; nature and culture. This bears similarities to an earlier list of *motivations* presented by Marilyn Hood (1983), in which she suggests six reasons why people visit museums (based on a wide-ranging review of the literature) and these were: being with other people,

Masberg and Silverman's Experiential Categories	*Hood's Reasons to Visit*
Companions	Being with people, or social interaction
Culture	Doing something worthwhile
Built Environment	Feeling comfortable and at ease in one's surroundings
Nature	Having a challenge of new experiences
Site Personnel	Having an opportunity to learn
Information	Participating actively
Activities	

Table 3.1 Masberg and Silverman's experiential categories (left) and Hood's reasons for visiting (right)

or having a social interaction; doing something worthwhile; feeling comfortable and at ease in one's surroundings; having the challenge of new experiences; having an opportunity to learn and participating actively in something (Hood, 1983). Although Hood's paper was written about museum visiting rather than visitor centres or heritage sites (as per Masberg and Silverman's paper) it does bear strong similarities to Masberg and Silverman's reported experiences of heritage sites and is therefore worth considering in conjunction with the other list (also, very little has been written directly on why people visit visitor centres). These categories are shown in Table 3.1.

What kinds of experiences are visitors having? Ousby observes, 'Tourists don't visit country houses or ruins or nature just for fun but out of the belief that the experience will in some way educate or uplift them' (Ousby, 2002, p. 9). In Masberg and Silverman's paper on visitors' experiences of heritage sites, they suggest that there are three kinds of outcomes that people are seeking, namely personal, emotional or experiential and by experiential they suggest that these are really aesthetic experiences, such as an appreciation of a beautiful atmosphere or the appearance of a place. These three categories (aesthetic, emotional or personal) are useful to consider, even if they are not entirely separate, since a visitor might have a strong emotional response to an experience that is primarily an aesthetic or personal one, and so we will briefly examine each of these in turn. In the next section it should be noted that these experiences (aesthetic, emotional or personal) can be of the attraction or resource but can also be of the visitor centre building and therefore both will be considered together.

Aesthetic outcomes

Aesthetics has a long history in architecture, going back to Vitruvius. Weber starts his book on the aesthetics of architecture with the question, 'Do beautiful buildings and spaces have something in common despite differences in function, appearance, style, manner of construction, environmental and cultural conditions? Do they share common qualities that trigger similar experiences and

judgements?' (Weber, 1995, p. 1). He then poses the question, '[are] aesthetic judgements … determined by characteristics of the object or by the viewer's own cognitive makeup?' (ibid., p. 4). This raises the most important consideration of work on aesthetics: *To what extent is our judgement a property of the object or the viewer?* And if it is entirely an individual response (i.e. there is no common agreement on what is 'beautiful'), it is still, nevertheless, the object – in this case the landscape, the visitor centre or the two combined – that is acting as a stimulus to this response. What exactly is the nature of this stimulus?

In architecture, writings on aesthetics tend to rapidly introduce terms such as 'proportion,' 'scale,' 'balance,' 'order,' 'symmetry,' and 'harmony,' often in a normative manner, explaining how one can use mathematics to design more aesthetically pleasing compositions. But this approach does not satisfy many critics and writers, Ernst Cassirer for example, suggests that it is fundamentally inadequate:

> Order, proportion, definite delimitation, and simple structure are usually taken as the characteristics of beautiful objects; yet these characteristics are obviously insufficient to comprehend all the elements which make up the aesthetically significant … as harmonious proportion and strict unity of form does not awaken in us the deepest emotions of the soul or the most intense artistic experiences. (Cassirer, 1951, p. 328)

If visitors to visitor centres are seeking aesthetic experiences or 'intense artistic experiences', to use Cassirer's phrase, are they likely to get these? I would suggest that they might. If we consider the full set of visitor centres featured in this book, then the picturesque ruins of Fountains Abbey or Whitby Abbey or the frenzy of intricate stone carvings inside Rosslyn Chapel are all examples of architectural places that might easily elicit a strong aesthetic response. Equally, in terms of landscape, the outstanding views of the Northumbrian National Park from The Sill visitor centre, or the geological spectacle that is the Giant's Causeway, may also provoke such a response. Many of the visitor centres, as buildings, can induce a strong aesthetic response, from the sensitive reuse of existing buildings, such as in the Whitby Abbey and Wycoller Aisled Barn visitor centres to the striking, sculptural forms of the glasshouses in the Bombay Sapphire visitor centre.

Emotional outcomes

An emotional experience is the next of Masberg and Silverman's three categories of outcomes that they suggest that visitors are seeking. So, how do we respond emotionally to a site or to a visitor centre building? I would suggest that we may have an emotional response either directly, as a result of some aspect of the outward appearance of a place, or indirectly, due to the instrinsic, cultural or historic significance of a setting.

Peter Zumthor describes how, on entering a room, he forms an immediate impression of the space's 'atmosphere' or 'quality': 'I enter a building, see a room, and – in a fraction of a second, have this feeling about it' (Zumthor, 2006, p. 13). What kinds of features of buildings might elicit an emotional response and what kinds of responses? Does architecture have the power to make us feel positive emotions such as calmness, contentment, delight, amusement, or curiosity? Most architectural theorists would concur that architecture (and landscape) does have the power to elicit an emotional response, but since these tend to be very individual reactions to a place, no direct causal relationship between specific architectural or landscape features and any such elicited emotions can be established. This does not, of course, mean that we might not experience a very powerful emotional response to the atmosphere of a site.

However, it is also clear that certain sites can produce a very strong emotional response simply due to their historic significance. The battlefield sites of Culloden and Bannockburn might produce strong emotional reactions. At Culloden this can be especially true of the inscribed stone of grave markers located around the site to commemorate Scottish clans and their clansmen (possibly all the stronger if the visitor happens to bear the same clan surname). Equally, the Mary Rose visitor centre might also

elicit an emotional response as, poignantly, so many crew perished as the ship went down – when people are viewing the now resurrected ship, they are also visiting a gravesite. Finally, many of the ecclesiastic sites also have the power to prompt a strong emotional response from their visitors, regardless of whether they share the same religious views, simply because of a recognition that these sites were once the receptacles of years of fervent prayers and beliefs. The challenge for the architect is to design the visitor centre *appropriately* so as to respect these kinds of emotional responses to the resource (and not to create a cognitive dissonance by invoking an entirely different set of emotional responses to the building).

Personal outcomes

What kinds of personal experiences or outcomes might people come away with (other than the aesthetic and emotional responses described above)? If the visitor is part of a group, then a satisfactory personal outcome might arise from a worthwhile social interaction with other members of the group. (And a well-designed visitor centre might very simply facilitate this through the design of intimate spaces conducive to such social interactions.) Another personal outcome might simply be the feeling of satisfaction or achievement at having tried a new activity or learnt something new, in other words, through some sort of personal 'growth' or development.

The personal outcome might also be due to some very individual link to the site. For me, visiting the Cutty Sark visitor centre in Greenwich was a deeply personal and emotional, experience as it was somewhere that my father, who had been long fascinated by the ship, had often taken me as a child. The day of my visit also happened to be close to the second anniversary of his death, and so the experience became an extremely personal and poignant one. Yet, this had nothing, intrinsically, to do with either the site, its setting, or the architecture of the visitor centre; no other visitor was likely to have had this self-same experience.

In this section we have looked at the visitor through history and tried to see if there are clues from the past that might explain the current

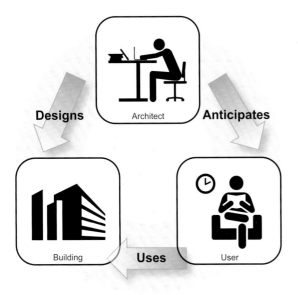

Figure 3.3 Relationship between the architect, the building and the bulding user
Source: Dalton and Hölscher (2016)

increase in popularity of the modern, British visitor centre. We have also tried to create a profile of a typical visitor and finally we have examined the motivations behind people's visits (focusing on aesthetic, emotional and personal outcomes).

Designing for the Visitor

The second part of this chapter concerns how the architect designing the visitor centre thinks of the visitor. How do they take the visitor's needs into account?

Figure 3.3 shows a diagram that Dalton and Hölscher have used in many of their joint publications, most recently in their book on the Seattle Central Library (2016). It illustrates how, when an architect is designing a building, they must do a number of things simultaneously: they must obviously design the building but also, in order to do this, they must at the same time, anticipate the actions and behaviours of the building user (for the sake of this chapter, *the visitor*, but this would also include the permanent staff working in the visitor centre): the visitor *uses* the building, the architect *designs* the building and the architect must also *anticipate* how the visitor uses the building. Initially this seems a fairly straightforward thing to do, but in reality it is both harder and more complex than might first be imagined and there are four stages to the process: imagining being inside an, as yet, un-built building (or inner spatial experiencing skills – defined in the following section); putting themselves into the shoes of their user (or perspective taking skills); discarding their own expert knowledge to better imitate the knowledge-state of a naïve, first time visitor and finally, to combine all of the above simultaneously. The next section will briefly expand upon all of these.

The first thing that an architect needs to do, during the design process, is to imagine being inside the unrealised visitor centre. To do this they need to be able to look at a two-dimensional drawing or sketch of a building and imagine themselves moving through and experiencing the corresponding three-dimensional space (in perspective vision). This is directly comparable to the way in which some musicians are able to sight read sheet music and imagine the music playing in their heads, known as 'inner hearing skills'. Given the analogy to music, this ability of some architects could, perhaps, be termed 'inner spatial-experiencing skills' (see Dalton, 2016). The architect Philip Johnson also promotes this activity; his advice to architects is that they should 'proceed on foot again and again through [their] imagined buildings. Then after months of approaching and re-approaching, and looking and turning, then only draw them up for the builder' (Johnson, 1965, p. 172).

Next, the architect needs to be able to put themselves into the shoes of the user. They need to imagine being inside the visitor's head and to try experiencing the building as if through their eyes. If the aspects of the building that we have described at the beginning of this chapter are so important to the visitor, namely, facilitating a comfortable visit, eliciting or creating memorable experiences, providing ample opportunities for fulfilling social interactions, learning something new and allowing people to feel in touch with something 'authentic', then how does an architect even begin to accommodate all of these requirements without getting into the shoes of the visitors? This act of being able to put yourself into the position of another person is what, in psychology, is known as 'perspective-taking' and I want to devote some time to presenting and discussing the concept.

The concept of perspective-taking (or being able to take another person's perspective) has been around since the 1930s and was, for example, discussed by Piaget (1932) in the context of his work on childhood developmental stages (Piaget describes the development of 'reciprocity' and 'the desire to treat others as he himself would wish to be treated' (ibid., p. 194). Such reciprocity requires a child to be able put him or herself into the place of an 'other'). This social ability is extremely useful for many tasks and situations since 'Well-developed perspective-taking abilities allow us to overcome our usual egocentrism ...' (Davis et al., 1996, p. 713) and, furthermore, 'Perspective taking allows an individual to anticipate the behavior and reactions of others' (Davis, 1983, p. 115). This is done best when they are able, in Davis's words, to overcome their usual egocentrism. And although this is rarely discussed in the context of architectural design or architectural education, this is clearly an example of perspective-taking as defined in the psychology literature. Perspective-taking is also strongly aligned to the more general ability to show empathy for others (and hence, in a design context, is plainly also associated with Empathic Design (Rayport and Leonard-Barton, 1997), sometimes mislabelled as Empathetic Design).

Tenbrink et al. (2014) suggest that highly skilled and experienced architects are able to employ both excellent 'perspective-taking' as well as outstanding 'inner spatial-experiencing skills' but that the hardest task of all is to simultaneously combine the two mental activities: to imagine yourself, *as someone else*, inhabiting an imaginary space. The reason why this is difficult for an architect is that it requires,

to some extent, being able to off-load or disregard their own expert knowledge in order to experience a building as a layperson. Also, since an architect who designs a building has an almost 'godlike' (at least omniscient if not omnipotent) knowledge of the project, how do they try to 'get in the shoes' of a naïve user, possibly visiting a building for the first time, without such a complete knowledge of it or even simply knowing what is around the next corner? In the previous chapter, there was a discussion of how to create a meaningful, affective experience for a visitor who is mostly likely a *first-time* visitor (and 59 per cent of people sampled by Dickinson et al. (2004) in the National Trust properties were first-time visitors). First-time visitors will arrive at a visitor centre, without any prior experience of the building. They will not know their way around the site and will need to be guided or oriented.

This trickier, combined activity of putting themselves into the shoes of the visitor, whilst simultaneously imagining inhabiting the, as yet, unrealised building is the final challenge. Perhaps we could call this empathic or reciprocal 'inner spatial-experiencing skills' or even 'third person-' as opposed to 'first person-inner spatial-experiencing skills. But whatever term we employ, if an architect wants to be able to design exceptional visitor centres, this is what they need to do. And, to harken back to Davis, this also requires them to suppress their own ego in order to achieve this (Davis, 1983). Needless to say, this is not an easy thing to do.

In this chapter we have looked at the visitor through history, some facts and statistics about the modern visitor and examined why it is that people are visiting these sites and attractions. We then briefly examined how an architect can best design for a meaningful and rich visitor experience and concluded the chapter by suggesting that this can only be achieved through empathy (putting themselves into the visitor's shoes), and by the suppression of ego.

4.
The Archetypal Visitor Centre

In Chapter 1 the question was asked whether the visitor centre might be a new type of building. The literature was reviewed on how building types emerge and how they are identified as 'new', with most theorists in agreement that new building types can only be identified once sufficient numbers have been built and studied in order to determine whether (or not) they share sufficient functional, formal and spatial characteristics. Therefore, in this chapter, we will attempt to do precisely this. The full set of visitor centres visited and studied for this book, including, wherever possible, those few that are still under construction or may have been closed, will be examined in order to determine what commonalities, if any, emerge from this analysis.

It is worth noting the comments by Stuart Evans, from the Northumberland National Park Authority, on the topic of whether it is possible to define a 'generic' visitor centre: 'How could you write a generic manual that says, "This is how you put a visitor centre on the top of a mountain" because there's one in Snowdonia. How do you do one that says, "Right, we're going to put one in a former clay pit"? They're very bespoke to their locations'. The implication, from his comments, is that the bespoke nature of visitor centre locations renders this task all but impossible, nevertheless, at the end of this chapter, it is hoped that an archetypal visitor centre can be defined and described (and therefore, it can be said, with some confidence, that visitor centres are a new building type).

Functional Characteristics

Let us begin with the functional attributes of the typical visitor centre. The definition of 'functional' is quite wide in the context of this investigation as it includes not only the kinds of 'functional' spaces which are included in our set of buildings, but also the 'themes' of the visitor centres, their age, costs and relative sizes. First, let us examine the reasons for which visitor centres have been created. What is the nature of the 'attraction' to which they facilitate visiting? For every visitor centre in this book, a series of tags were devised: words that are intended to capture and categorise the visitor centre's 'attraction' or 'resource', for example:

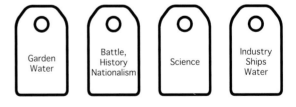

Figure 4.1 Tags for: Alnwick Gardens; Bannockburn; Jodrell Bank; the Titan Crane visitor centres (as read left to right)

For reference, the tag information is also included in the *key facts* section for the twenty visitor centres showcased in the following case study chapters. Once these themes had been established for each visitor centre, it was possible to determine whether any patterns or overarching themes emerged. The diagram shown in Figure 4.2 presents the outcome of this analysis, whereby each 'bubble' in the diagram contains the visitor centres which share that thematic theme, for example Fountains Abbey, Rosslyn Chapel and Whitby Abbey visitor centres are all connected by sharing the tag 'religion'. Equally the Cutty Sark, the Mary Rose and the Titan Crane visitor centres are all connected by having something to do with ships and shipping (the Cutty Sark and the Titan Crane visitor centres are further connected via the tag, 'Industry/Commerce', whereas the Mary Rose could not be described by this tag). In Figure 4.2 the size of the circle represents the total number of visitor centres that share a specific theme and so it can easily be seen that the largest theme is 'water', followed by 'landscape and geology' and 'archaeology and ruins' being the third largest category. Many themes are closely related, for example, water and wildlife (Brockholes and Welney Wetland visitor centres are examples of sites in which water and wildlife clearly intersect).

Other larger groupings of themes also emerged, for example water, shipping and industry can be seen to be a clear cluster. If we were to ask the question of where the archetypal visitor centre would be located, the answer would be rural since 79 per cent of visitor centres are classified as being rural in this sample (19 per cent are urban and 2 per cent are coastal), and so 'water', 'wildlife' and 'landscape/geology' are clearly some of the key themes that might be expected to be found in a predominantly rural location, as might archaeology/ruins. Thematically, visitor centres such as the Giant's Causeway, Stonehenge and The Sill can be seen as being particularly representative of the typical 'thematic' visitor centre.

Are there any patterns that emerge with respect to *when* the visitor centre has been built? In Chapters 1 and 3 it was suggested that visitor centres have become far more popular recently and that most of the architectural award-winning visitor centres date from the early 1990s onwards. Is there a particular time period with which visitor centres can be associated? If we look at Figure 4.3, it is clear that the number of visitor centres being built every year has increased, is still rising, and that they do not yet appear to have 'peaked' (despite the fact that the potential market for new visitor centres must be finite since visitor centres are rarely created where there is not already an attraction to which visitors are already visiting). Therefore, in terms of a temporal pattern, we can say little other than numbers constructed are still increasing.

If we next examine the typical cost of a visitor centre, there is considerable variation, with some notable examples at either extreme end of the scale. At the most expensive end are visitor centres such as Hafod Eryri (on top of Snowdon), Whitby Abbey and Rosslyn Chapel (costing, on average, £10,300 per square metre – adjusted for inflation due to different construction dates), and at the bottom end are some of the smallest visitor centres, for example the Titan Crane and Wycoller Aisled Barn visitor centres (which demonstrates that high quality, award-winning architecture can come in the very smallest of packages). The average cost for the visitor centres featured in this book is £5,240 per square metre (adjusted for the date of construction) and approximately half of all the visitor centres are within £1,700/m^2 (plus or minus) of this figure. (Given that there is 25 years' difference between the earliest and most recent visitor centre in this book, costs for this exercise were adjusted for inflation and so the costs per square metre are not the actual costs provided by the architects for the year of construction but represent what those costs would be today (see www.measuringworth.com)).

Any discussion of costs and costs per square metre could not begin without touching briefly upon the question of overall size of a visitor centre. As suggested above, there are certainly very large and very small visitor centres (the largest is The Sill visitor centre at 2,900m^2 and the smallest in the sample is the Titan Crane visitor centre at 64m^2 – 45 Titan Crane visitor centres would fit inside The Sill), but is there a typical size of visitor centre?

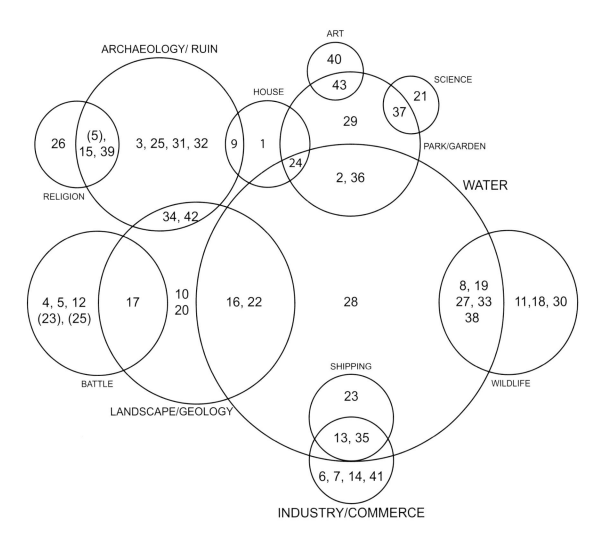

ART

ARCHAEOLOGY/ RUIN

HOUSE

SCIENCE

40

43

21

37

29

26

(5),
15, 39

3, 25, 31, 32

9

1

PARK/GARDEN

24

2, 36

WATER

RELIGION

34, 42

4, 5, 12
(23), (25)

17

10
20

16, 22

28

8, 19
27, 33
38

11,18, 30

BATTLE

SHIPPING

WILDLIFE

LANDSCAPE/GEOLOGY

23

13, 35

6, 7, 14, 41

INDUSTRY/COMMERCE

1 Abbotsford
2 Alnwick Gardens
3 Archaeolink
4 Bannockburn
5 Battle of Hastings
6 Beefeater Gin
7 Bombay Saphire
8 Brockholes
9 Chedworth Roman Villa
10 Chiltern Hills Gateway
11 Coedwig Coed Y Brenin
12 Culloden Battlefield
13 Cutty Sark
14 David Mellor
15 Fountains Abbey

16 Giants Causeway
17 Glencoe
18 Glentress
19 Great Fen
20 Hafod Eryri
21 Jodrell Bank
22 Loch Lomond Gateway
23 Mary Rose
24 Millfield House
25 Richard III
26 Rosslyn Chapel
27 RSPB Saltholme
28 Samphire Hoe
29 Savill Garden
30 Sherwood Forest

31 Stonehenge
32 Sutton Hoo
33 Swansea Bay
34 The Sill
35 Titan Crane
36 Virginia Water
37 Wakehurst Place
38 Welney Wildfowl
39 Whitby Abbey
40 Window on Mackintosh
41 Woodhorn Colliery
42 Wycoller Aisled Barn
43 Yorkshire Sculpture Park

**Figure 4.2 Diagram of tag associations of
visitor centres**

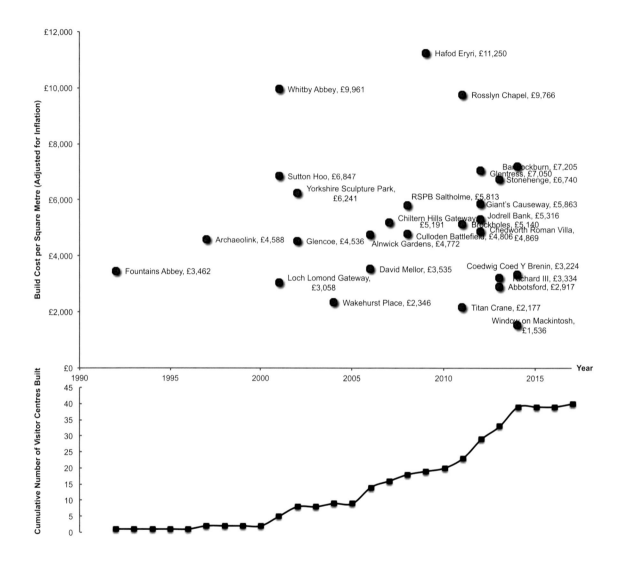

Figure 4.3 The historic economic cost
(above) and the cumulative total (below)
of award-winning visitor centres built
between 1990–2017

Figure 4.4 illustrates the footprints of many of the visitor centres featured in this book, all drawn to the same scale. It is clear that there is a wide range and variation in overall size and that no commonalities exist. The average size, however, can be calculated to be 1,555m². So what determines the size of the visitor centre? It is most likely that this is dictated by the visitor numbers (past and projected). In terms of visitor numbers, we were able to establish numbers for almost 40 per cent of the visitor centres studied. Of these, the range is also considerable with Stonehenge receiving 1,366,765 visitors[1] in 2015 and Titan Crane 3,000 visitors.[2] The average number, across all visitor centres, for which data was available, is approximately 300,000 visitors per year.

In terms of what are the functional sub-spaces found within a visitor centre, the most typical sub-spaces to be found in a visitor centre are: a welcome/ticketing area; a cafe or restaurant; a shop; toilets; exhibition or information/orientation area or a gallery; a flexible space, community space or school/classroom space; and staff/administrative offices (and other 'back-of-house' subsidiary areas), see Chapter 1, Figure 1.2. Obviously, in different visitor centres, the inclusion of and amount of space given to these different areas is different. One example is the prominence given to the welcome desk/ticketing area: almost all visitor centres have this, but one notable exception is Wycoller Aisled Barn visitor centre, which is unmanned and therefore a welcome desk would be unnecessary. Hafod Eryri, the visitor centre located at the summit of Snowdon is also one that dispenses with the luxury of a welcome desk. Given these outliers, the most typical, four functional subspaces in a visitor centre tend to be the welcome area, the shop, the cafe and the exhibition area. To show how these vary, see Figure 4.5 for a series of pie charts, showing the relative split between these four functions (the other spaces are excluded for the sake of this exercise, in order to render them more comparable). These charts show that, on average, the welcome area is allocated the smallest area (clearly, it may only be as small as the immediate standing-space in front of the welcome desk, if a welcome desk is included) and that the cafe and the shop tend to be of equal size and that

any exhibition/gallery area tends to be conferred the largest space. We can calculate an average size for all these functions, across all of the visitor centres studied (and for which areas could be calculated) and these are the: shop at 103m²; cafe or restaurant = 110m²; exhibition or gallery area = 189m²; welcome desk/reception area = 39m². In the next section, on spatial characteristics, we can examine how these different functional areas of the visitor centres are related to each other spatially.

Spatial Characteristics

Let us now consider the spatial characteristics of the visitor centre. In the section above, it was clear that the most frequently included functional sub-spaces are the cafe, shop, welcome area and exhibition areas, but we did not explore the spatial relationship between these sub-spaces. One way of considering how these spaces are organised or arranged into the archetypal visitor centre is to consider the relationships between the spaces. It is possible to create a graph of the spaces within a building, formed by considering each separate space as a node in the graph and, if it is possible to move directly from one space (or node) to another space (or node) without passing through any intermediate spaces, then we can say that these spaces are connected and represent this relationship by a link in the graph. Once all spaces in the visitor centre have been represented in this manner, we can reorganise the resultant graph, from the perspective of the external space (which is also represented as a node in the graph). Every space that is connected to the outside is placed at one level away from the entrance, spaces connected to these are placed two levels away and so on, until all spaces have been ranked with respect to their distance from the outside. The resultant graph is known as a justified graph (and is one of the representations developed as part of the wider set of methods used in space syntax analysis). The justified graphs for the visitor centres (for which we had sufficient information about the function of spaces) are shown in Figure 4.6. All spaces are shown here and the

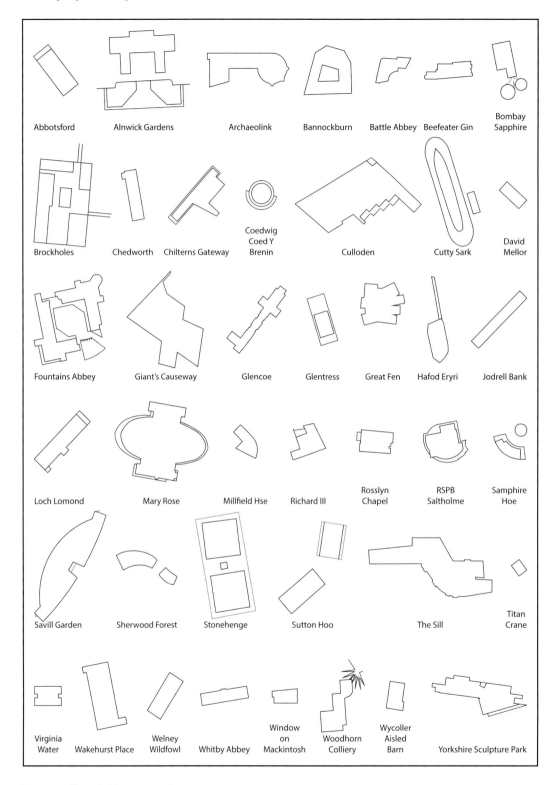

Figure 4.4 Sizes of visitor centres, drawn to the same scale
Source: The author and Danilo di Mascio

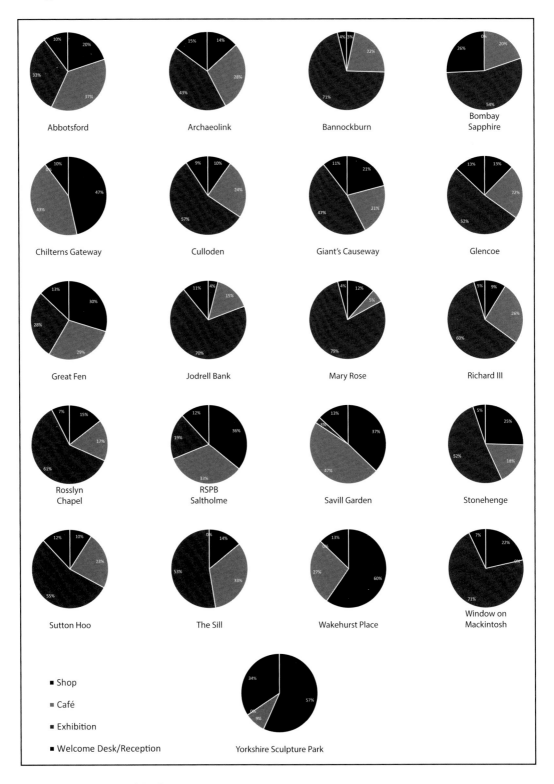

Figure 4.5 Relative areas of the shop, cafe, exhibition and welcome spaces for a selection of visitor centres
Source: The author and Danilo di Mascio

welcome area (labelled 'W'), the cafe space (labelled 'C'), the shop (labelled 'S') and the exhibition/gallery space (labelled 'E') are indicated by the labels on the graphs.

What is clear, looking at these graphs, is they are all surprisingly deep (so that in order to visit all of the parts of the visitor centre, the visitor has to penetrate into the depths of the building). Not surprisingly the welcome desk/welcome area is usually one of the spaces most accessible from the outside, and therefore is typically either directly connected to the outside (level 1) or no more than one step-depth away from it (level 2). Where the welcome desk/ticketing area is located at two spatial steps away from the outside, it is typically where the design includes some kind of intermediate entrance space/lobby prior to moving into the main building (where the second space to be encountered is the welcome desk). On average the welcome area is located at a depth of 1.8 spaces from the outside. The next most easily reached space from the outside is the shop (its average depth from the outside is 2.3 spaces), which is often co-located with the welcome/ticketing desk (but typically set slightly beyond/behind it). Again, this makes intuitive sense for if the business model of the visitor centre is to increase revenue via the shop, then to maximise spend, this should be the last space the visitor encounters on leaving the visitor centre. If it is the last place to pass through, then its spatial relationship to the outside must be close. The cafe tends to be about 3 spatial steps away from the outside, so still relatively close (average is 3.4). This is close enough to the outside and to the entry space so that visitors who simply want to come in and use the cafe only, can do so without having to move around the rest of the building. There is some variation of the depth of the cafe though, with spatially 'deeper' cafes either being located on the second floor (and hence more circulation spaces need to be negotiated in order to reach it) as in the case of RSPB Saltholme's visitor centre or it is the case that the 'deeper' cafes tend to be more of a 'restaurant/dining' experience than a cafe (as in the case of Abbotsford's or Savill Garden's restaurants).

Given that all of the three spaces above (welcome area, shop and cafe) are relatively closely clustered around the entrance/exit to the outside, the spatial relationship between the outside and the exhibition space is quite different. The exhibition spaces are typically located far deeper into the building, often occupying some of the deepest places, those furthest from the entrance space. The average number of steps from the entrance to the outside is 4.2 steps, but many visitor centres have exhibition spaces that are, on average, far deeper than this. Although, those visitor centres that have the 'deepest' exhibitions also tend to be those where the distinction between visitor centre and museum is the hardest to establish, for example the Richard III visitor centres (average exhibition step depth of 6.43 spatial steps) or the Mary Rose museum/visitor centre (average exhibition depth is 7.40 steps away). Another interesting spatial characteristic of the exhibition spaces, is that they tend not to be a single space but rather a cluster of spaces that form an entire spatial sub-complex. These sets of spaces are typically quite distinct from the rest of the building, and have their own internal spatial logic and narrative sequence.

Another way of considering the spatial layout of a visitor centre is to search for what, in space syntax terms, is called an 'inequality genotype' (Hillier et al., 1987; Bafna, 2001). A 'genotype' is essentially a sort of spatial 'thumbprint' for a specific building type and is derived by ordering labelled spaces from the most public (or spatially 'integrated' locations) to the most private (the spatially segregated locations) and seeing if the same pattern, or sequence, of spaces, ranked in this way, reoccurs in multiple buildings of the same type. If this repeated, ranked pattern emerges from the analysis of many buildings, then the presence of such an 'inequality genotype' is indicative this this is a distinct building type (Hillier et al.). If we consider only the labelled spaces, the welcome desk (W), shop (S), cafe (C) and exhibition spaces (E), the integration value for each space in the graph (integration is a measure of how accessible, public and central versus inaccessible, private and peripheral is a space, ibid.) can be calculated. If we consider Abbotsford visitor centre as an example, the integration values of the relative named spaces are: welcome desk area is 0.986; the shop is 1.303; the cafe is 2.027 and the exhibition

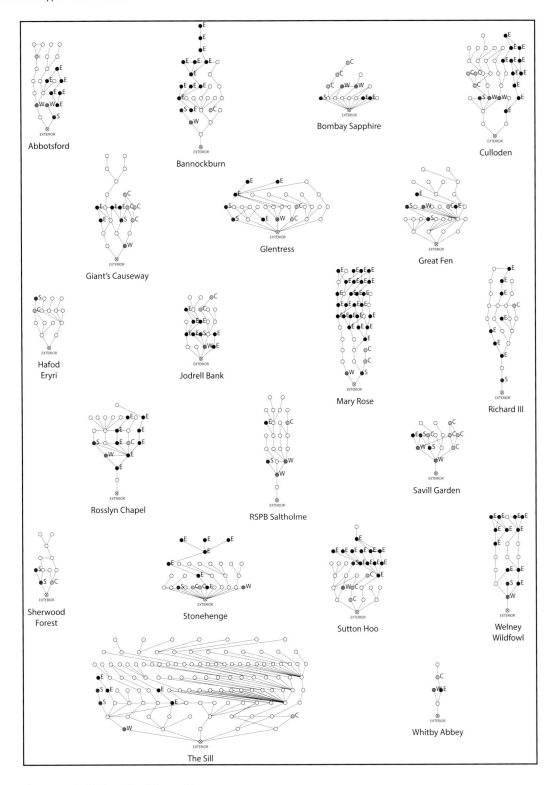

Figure 4.6 Justified graphs of the spatial networks of a selection of visitor centres
Source: The author and Danilo di Mascio

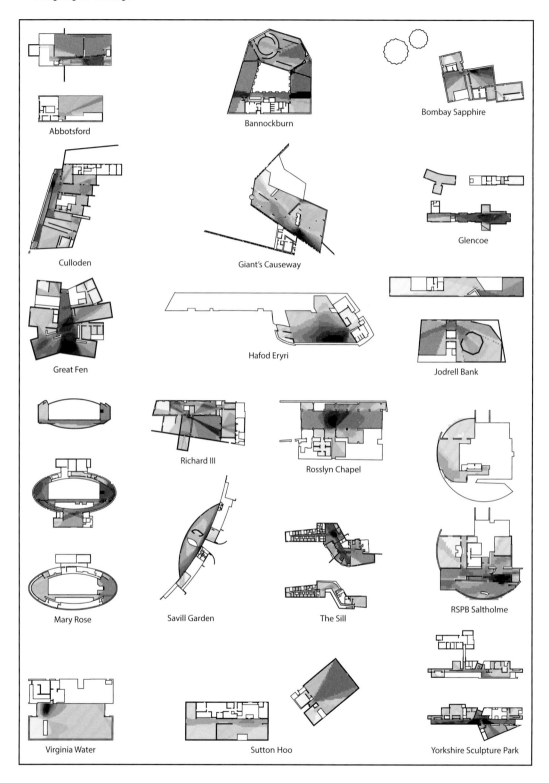

Figure 4.7 Spatial analyses of a selection of visitor centres (visibility graph analysis: dark grey = most integrated spaces; light grey = most segregated spaces)

areas are, on average, 1.584. The lower the value the higher the integration value and the more public/accessible/integrated is the space. Therefore, to rank these in order, we get the sequence, 'W, S, E, C' (ordered from the most public to the most private). Although the exact values vary, this same sequence of *Welcome area < Shop < Exhibition < Cafe* is shared by, for example, the Bombay Sapphire visitor centre and the Jodrell Bank visitor centre, to name but two. This is clearly very similar, in sequence to 'W, S, C, E', in which the welcome desk and the shop are still the two most integrated areas (and in that order), but in this ordering, the cafe and the exhibition areas are swapped around. This is a sequence of spatial ranking shared by, for example, Bannockburn, Culloden and Savill Garden visitor centres. In fact, these two variations account for over half of all visitor centres (with the 'W, C, S, E' being the next most popular ordering). On this basis, it can be suggested that *there is a spatial genotype for visitor centres*, but that is it split into two sub-variations, those where the exhibition is more segregated ('W, S, C, E') and

those where the cafe is more segregated ('W, S, E, C'). As for the j-graphs, the latter variant probably consists of visitor centres where the cafe is on the second floor or if it is a more 'fine dining' type of restaurant (see Figure 4.7).

At a completely different spatial scale of analysis, in Chapter 1 it was suggested that the relationship between the visitor centre building and the attraction could take on a number of different modes: the attraction inside the visitor centre; the attraction being semi-enclosed by the visitor centre; the attraction adjacent to or touching the visitor centre; the attraction near to the visitor centre; the attractions distant from the visitor centre and the attraction surrounding the visitor centre. Again, if we consider all 43 visitor centres we can determine whether there is a predominant spatial relationship between the visitor centre building and the attraction. From Figure 4.8 we can see that most visitor centres are either surrounded by their attraction (Hafod Eryri visitor centre is on top of and is surrounded by Snowdon Mountain) or is near to its attraction (i.e.

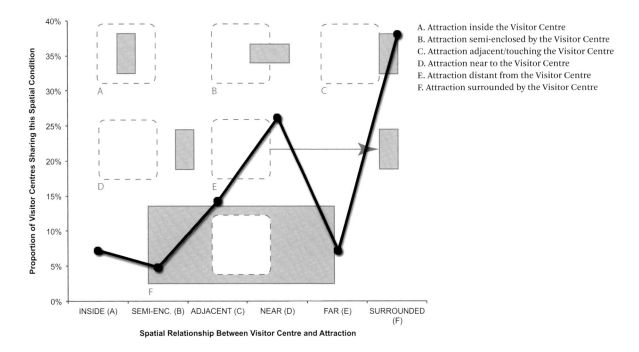

A. Attraction inside the Visitor Centre
B. Attraction semi-enclosed by the Visitor Centre
C. Attraction adjacent/touching the Visitor Centre
D. Attraction near to the Visitor Centre
E. Attraction distant from the Visitor Centre
F. Attraction surrounded by the Visitor Centre

Figure 4.8 Spatial relationship between visitor centre and its attraction or resource

Bannockburn, Jodrell Bank and Whitby Abbey are all examples of this spatial relationship). These two spatial conditions combined account for 62 per cent of all visitor centres. The more unusual spatial conditions are for the attraction to be 'inside' the visitor centre (7.1 per cent), to be semi-enclosed by it (4.8 per cent), far away from it (7.1 per cent) or adjacent to it (14.3 per cent); see Figure 4.8.

Formal Characteristics

In this last section we will consider whether there are certain formal, rather than spatial or functional, characteristics shared by all or many of the visitor centres. One starting point is simply to define a set of characteristics, which may be internal or external elements, they may be structural, formal, compositional, stylistic or materialistic, and then to determine how frequently these occur. Initially, a 'scheme' (basically a checklist of features) was produced and each of the 43 visitor centres was then examined to determine which of the formal characteristics or formal elements, if any, they contained. (In reality, this scheme was developed through a more *iterative process* of observing prominent building features during visits, amending the feature-set, re-mapping the adjusted features to the buildings and continuing this until the list of features or characteristics stabilised). The frequency with which these features are found in visitor centres can be plotted on a graph, see Figure 4.9. It is immediately clear from this figure that a number of these elements appear to be featured in many visitor centres. From this figure, we can see immediately that the most common, formal elements are: being a single-storey building; framing views and having strong formal symmetries; quirky, or idiosyncratic rooflines; bridges; canopies or use of 'vernacular' materials such as wood and stone. In the following section we will briefly examine and discuss a selection of these, in turn.

It should, however, be noted that there is no attempt, in this next section, to be prescriptive. Simply because these formal elements have been observed in many architecturally significant visitor centres, it does not mean that a visitor centre has to feature one or more of these features. At the same time, it should also be noted that while certain elements do appear to crop up regularly, that simply including one of these building-elements does not indicate that the building *has to be* a visitor centre (in contrast to the way that a spire is normally indicative of a building being a church or a minaret indicative of a building being a mosque). It would surely be nonsensical to suggest that every single-storey building, with a bridge leading to it, and a quirky roofline must, by definition, be a visitor centre. It is, nonetheless, still an interesting exercise to examine these features, since the outward appearance or a building is core to the academic foundations of typology.

Quirky Rooflines

Why should quirky rooflines be one of the formal characteristics of visitor centres? This could result from the influence of two different aspects of the design of visitor centres. First, visitor centres are typically not so large as to need two storeys of accommodation and so most of them are single-storey (which also helps to reduce the visual impact in what is often a predominantly rural context); second, there is a pull towards trying to design something that is *distinctive* and so, it could be argued, does justice to its 'exceptional setting'. The architectural design problem is therefore one of how do you make a low, single-storey building, stand out from other buildings and have an identifiable character of its own? (See the section in Chapter 2 for a full discussion of iconic, invisible and synergistic buildings). The use of quirky rooflines are therefore a means by which the visitor centre may be able to stand out from its neighbouring, everyday (often rural, vernacular) buildings, and seem somewhat 'distinctive' without being overly attention-seeking. The roofline may also provide an opportunity to make a symbolic reference to the visitor centre's purpose. Therefore, the very distinctive roofline at Woodhorn Museum and Northumberland Archives takes its inspiration from coal-cutting machinery, and the cantilevered, petal-shaped roof canopies at

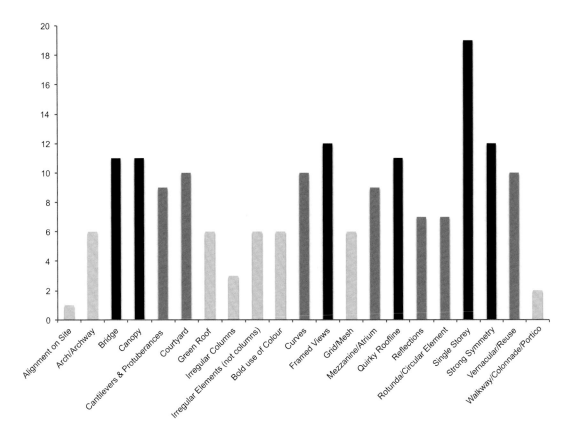

Figure 4.9 Occurrence of formal elements (darker colour = higher frequency of feature)

RSPB Saltholme are reminiscent of birds' wings in flight. The Project Architect of The Sill visitor centre, Alison Thornton-Sykes, had this to say about the design of the roof of The Sill:

> The roofs over The Sill [are] reflective of natural forms, which would be more cantilevered, rather than being pegged down. In the nature of a can-tilever, it has an energy and a movement about it. I think they're not static places, are they? They're about movement, and moving on to the next thing. I think you want the building somehow to express that.

Bridges

Bridges are a particularly interesting feature that many visitor centres share. They can serve one of three design purposes and frequently may combine two or even all three functions in a single visitor centre. At a most pragmatic level, bridges are clearly useful for overcoming obstacles (for example, bridging over the New Bedford River, in the case of Welney visitor centre), accommodating changes in site-levels (Whitby Abbey visitor centre) or simply making the 'attraction' more accessible, especially to wheelchairs (the Cutty Sark visitor centre). Second, bridges can be a useful control mechanism, espe-cially in sites where tickets are a requirement. If the only way to access a site is via a bridge and the only

**Figure 4.10 The roof at Woodhorn Museum
inspired by coal-cutting machinery**

way to gain access to the bridge is with a ticket, then ticket-evasion becomes difficult, if not impossible. Finally, bridges have always had a symbolic nature, particularly in storytelling and mythology. Bridges are symbolic of leaving one world behind and entering a new one. And so perhaps, the number of bridges in visitor centres are also symbolic of the visitor leaving behind their everyday world and ensuring that they are in a mood to be receptive to the new ideas, knowledge and experiences waiting for them on the other side of the bridge.

Again, returning to Alison Thornton-Sykes, Project Architect of The Sill, and also Project Architect of another visitor centre researched in this book, RSPB Saltholme. When asked about the bridges in the RSPB Saltholme project, she had the following observations to make about them.

[The bridges originated from] a practical, anti-vandalism point of view, where they can [close] it, almost like a drawbridge. It was quite important, the idea behind Saltholme, to feel almost like a bird perched in this reed-bed landscape, with the landscape and water wrapping right around it, almost like an island, as well. I suppose [a bridge] also signifies that transition point, doesn't it? 'Well, now you're moving into something different.' I think [bridges] are quite exciting – you're leaving one world, and moving into another, it creates that gateway, [a] processional approach, doesn't it? And they're quite exciting structures, I think, bridges, generally. Again, it's that feeling of something that isn't quite pegged down; that is quite elevated, and just lightly touches the ground on both ends. With 'The Sill', the building is a contrast, in many ways, because you've got it very embedded in the earth at the entrance point (you want that sense of being really part of the geology). Then, it's about that movement away from that, really. I think [its forms] are quite expressive of movement and moving onto the next thing.

Canopies and Cantilevers
Cantilevers and canopies are undoubtedly connected to the 'quirky rooflines' as described above,

since many of the visitor centres with quirky or idiosyncratic rooflines could also be described as having prominent cantilevers or other such protuberances. Canopies and walkways are slightly different, and many visitor centres include covered walkways. Again, these may purely be a functional device, after all, Britain does not have the most temperate climate and where it is necessary to move from one building (or one part of a building) to another, to be able to do so in the relative comfort and shelter of a covered walkway and not get wet is clearly beneficial. Again, however, some of the covered walkways may also serve a symbolic function (as with the bridges) for example in the case of Fountains Abbey visitor centre, where the covered arcade is clearly symbolic of a monastic cloister.

Framed Views
Framed views are another common feature of visitor centres, which is hardly surprising given the frequently strong relationship between the visitor centre, the surrounding landscape and the attraction or resource. The client of The Sill visitor centre, Stuart Evans, emphasised, 'You want people to view things, and I think a lot of visitor centres are probably saying, "Right, how do we get people to look out as well as look in to the centre?"'. Many architects design the visitor centre to help orient the visitor towards specific views in the landscape. This may be to give tantalising glimpses, at a distance, of their destination, in the way that part of the building has been cut away in the Fountains Abbey visitor centre to provide views towards the top of the abbey tower. Sometimes, it may be because specific vantage points are provided to give an overview of the site, as in the case of Culloden's rooftop, a lookout point that permits elevated views across the battlefield site. Other examples include the Welney visitor centre, with its large picture windows, providing views over the Fens or, finally, for The Sill visitor centre, with its roof garden walk designed to incrementally focus the visitors' attention towards the rocks and skyline of The Whin Sill. The unique way in which the building of The Sill visitor centre helps to frame people's views towards the geological features of the setting is described in greater detail (as well as the

**Figure 4.11 A bridge in the Cutty Sark
visitor centre**

ways in which she tried to frame views in other visitor centres) by the architect Alison Thornton-Sykes:

The Sill [frames views]: that journey up the roof, the reason it's at its angle in that landscape is to align that final view, both from the cafe at the first-floor level, and from the roof level, to capture that view of the Great Whin Sill, with Hadrian's Wall … Then, on a softer front, the classroom is oriented to the south side of the garden, so they take in softer, gentler views. We've taken the same approach at RSPB Saltholme, where there was a long atrium route – we've got a long vista through the building, with the lake at the end. And in RSPB Sherwood (which we're working on at the minute), again, it takes the visitor journey from a village setting out to Sherwood Forest. It's an undulating form, but the end vista, a tall wall of glass at the end, has a front-on view of the old forest. So, absolutely, [we used framed views], in many ways, they're a starting point for how the building is configured and orientated on the site.

Materials

Given that 79 per cent of visitor centres in this book are set in rural contexts and, in addition to this, many of them are located in conservation areas, World Heritage Sites or Sites of Special Scientific Interest (Relph's 'exceptional settings'), it is perhaps unsurprising that many visitor centres should have adopted a material palette and language that could best be described as an understated or minimalist, neo-vernacular. Wood, as both a structural material and as an external cladding material is particularly common in visitor centres (two particularly good examples of exquisitely detailed and sensitive wooden cladding are to be found in Welney and Chedworth Roman Villa visitor centres). In many of the projects the timber has either been taken from sustainable sources or local ones, or both (sometimes even from the same estate as the visitor centre, as in the case of the Savill Garden visitor centre). Equally, stone features strongly in the set of materials used in the visitor centres. Hafod Eryri, where each stone had to be shaped and pre-assembled (and then disassembled

again) off-site before being taken up to the top of Snowdon by train is a wonderful example of a building whose materiality is paramount to the look and feel of the visitor centre. The Giant's Causeway and The Sill visitor centres, both about geological phenomena and hence each attempting to incorporate local igneous stone (basalt and dolerite stone respectively) into their building designs are also two excellent examples of buildings where the stone is of utmost importance.

Having considered and discussed the most common, formal elements to be found in visitor centres (such as framing views; quirky, or idiosyncratic rooflines; bridges; canopies or the use of specific building materials) it can be stated that the formal, material and visual appearances of many of the visitor centres in this book do share identifiable commonalities, but that this should not be considered either prescriptive (all visitor centres *have* to include these) nor indicative (buildings containing these elements *need not* necessarily be a visitor centre).

Summary

In this chapter we set out to see if we could identify what an archetypal visitor centre would be like, based on observed and calculated functional, spatial and formal similarities between the 43 visitor centres studied. As a result, a summary can be provided which describes what an *archetypal visitor centre* would look like:

With respect to functional considerations, it can be said that the average visitor centre has been constructed in the last ten years (and most probably built since 2010), is located in a rural setting and has a theme or focus around water and wildlife, landscape/geology or archaeology/ruins. Its construction cost is likely to be approximately £5,240 per square metre, but there is no typical size and indeed sizes vary considerably (probably depending upon past, or predicted, visitor numbers). The most typical functional spaces to be included in a visitor centre are the welcome desk, cafe, shop and exhibition area, with the cafe and shop being of equivalent sizes, the exhibition area typically being the size of the cafe and shop combined and the welcome desk being as small as possible to fulfil any essential welcoming and ticketing functions. The archetypal visitor centre would attract, on average, 300,000 visitors per year (based on the VisitEngland figures from 2015) and is more likely to be located in a rural rather than in an urban or coastal area.

It appears that many visitor centres feature similar spatial characteristics. First, it is likely that the relationship between the visitor centre and its associated attraction is most likely to be one where the visitor centre is either surrounded by its attraction (most typical if this attraction is a landscape or geological feature) or is near to it (when it is not a landscape). Second, for the majority of visitor centres, there is a strong spatial relationship between the welcome/ticketing area and the shop, both of which are located close to the outside and in close proximity to each other. Furthermore, it is typically the exhibition or gallery areas of the visitor centre that are both more spatially complex (often forming distinct spatial sub-clusters) and located further, or spatially deeper, inside the building (with the exception of two-storey buildings that have their cafe/restaurant on the second floor). The welcome desk is, on average, the most integrated space in the building and the exhibition spaces (taken together) are the most segregated (but a spatial variant of the spatial genotype occurs in some building where the cafe is the most segregated space).

In terms of the outward appearance, there are observed formal, compositional and material commonalities to be found in the set of visitor centres and so it can be suggested that many visitor centres appear to conform loosely to an identifiable, visual 'type' despite striving hard for their own individuality. The archetypal visitor centre is therefore a single-storey building, often with strong formal symmetries and a quirky, or idiosyncratic roof (which may symbolically connect to the theme of the visitor centre). Formally, bridges and canopies are the most striking visual feature of our archetypal visitor centre. Due to its rural location, the use of wood and stone (most likely to have been locally sourced) tend to be the most dominant materials, permitting the visitor centre to fit in with any vernacular

buildings in the area (but typically designed with a meticulous attention to detail unlikely to be found in any functional, vernacular building). Finally, the relationship between the building and the landscape is most likely expressed (aside from the materials used) through the ways in which the building helps to frame views to the landscape, helping the visitors orient themselves and focus on the wider context. However, despite the fact that we can identify such formal and visual characteristics and use them to define a *theoretic*, archetypal visitor centre, it is not intended that these observations be prescriptive of how *all* visitor centres should be designed, since a certain degree of distinctiveness or idiosyncrasy is also important to the design of a visitor centre. It is probably useful to end this chapter with a quote from Ivor Crowther of the Heritage Lottery Fund, commenting on the design of visitor centres:

> First of all, the building's got to be functional. It's got to meet the needs of the services that are going to be delivered from it. It's got to be appropriately sized for the audiences that are going to use the facility. I think we're fairly open on design. We're open to new concepts of design and new ways of thinking and working.

Equally, the nearest neighbour to The Sill visitor centre made this comment on the final appearance of the building, 'if it had been much more daring and risky – and I don't know what I'm thinking about, some glass bowl or whatever – I still think it's something one could do, as long as it's well designed'. So, if the funders are happy to explicitly state that they are 'fairly open on design', and if the community are also willing to entertain buildings that are 'much more daring and risky' as long as they are well designed, then architects need not feel overly constrained by the formal regularities of the precedent case studies observed in this chapter.

In conclusion, however, can we now say with confidence, that a new building type has emerged? Given the preceding analyses and observations, I would strongly suggest that we could.

top: Abbotsford visitor centre's entrance
and first floor balcony/restaurant terrace

above: Brockholes, showing the overall
massing of the buildings on the pontoon

**top: Bombay Sapphire's botanical
glasshouses**

**above: Bannockburn, showing the rear
façade and cafe windows**

**right: Alnwick Garden Pavilion showing the
lattice-shell roof structure**

**Culloden Battlefield showing one of the
dramatic, curved shell roofs above the
cafe/multi-functional spaces**

top: Chedworth Roman Villa showing the
entrance and ambulatory (corridor), left,
and interpretation room, right

above: Chiltern Hills Gateway showing its
unique aerofoil roof

**View of roof, balustrading and main façade
of the Giant's Causeway Visitor Centre**
Source: Heneghan Peng Architects,
photograph by Hufton & Crow

Fountains Abbey showing part of the
courtyard and surrounding seating

top: Interior, 'Welcome to Hafod Eryri'   above: Space Pavilion, Jodrell Bank: a black box in the landscape

top: Richard III visitor centre, frameless glazed viewing gallery, looking out over the courtyard

above: Rosslyn Chapel, showing the formal relationship between the new visitor centre and the eighteenth-century stable building

Interior, Stonehenge visitor centre
exhibition area showing part of a circular,
projected diorama of the stones

The Sill's façade facing The Whin Sill, showing its inclined rooftop vantage point

Photograph of the interior of the Titan
Crane visitor centre and the base of the
Titan Crane beyond

Welney Wetland Centre looking from the
upper, to the lower, roof terrace

top: Interior, Whitby Abbey visitor centre
looking towards the abbey ruins

above: Interior, Wycoller Aisled Barn with
glass 'pod'

Case Studies

Abbotsford

KEY FACTS

FULL NAME

Abbotsford Visitor Centre

ARCHITECTS

LDN Architects

COMPLETION DATE

2013

COST

£3,200,000

COST/m²

£2,714

NEAREST POSTCODE

TD6 9BQ

SELECTED AWARDS

Scottish Design Awards, Sustainable Design Award – Winner 2013

Scottish Design Awards, Best Public Building – Commendation 2013

RIAS – Highly Commended 2013

RIAS Forestry Commission Special Prize 2013

RIAS Best Use of Wood 2013

House
Writer
Culture
Nationalism

Abbotsford visitor centre showing the scale
of its large canopy roof

For many people (both Scots and non-Scots alike) Sir Walter Scott's writings epitomise a romantic view of an historic Scotland. Famous novels written by him include *Ivanhoe*, *Rob Roy*, *The Lady of the Lake*, *Waverley* and *The Bride of Lammermoor*, and he has frequently been named the originator of the historical novel. Although a lawyer by profession, relatively early in his life he became fascinated by the oral folk stories of the Scottish Borders and started to collect these Border tales (which he later published). Out of this love for the Border histories, ballads and stories he developed his own explorations and reimaginings of Scottish history. These in turn, captured the public's imagination and eventually fuelled a revival in all things Scottish. For Scott, however, his love for the Scottish Borders and for Scottish history were inextricably bound with his love for his home, Abbotsford, the house that he built on the banks of the River Tweed.

Abbotsford House is a singularly unusual house, originally the site of a farmhouse, Scott gradually added to, and refined it until the house resembled an assemblage of stone and brick, towers and turrets, roofs and stepped-gables; it could be considered to lie somewhere between the picturesque and the eccentrically quirky. The estate in which the house lies is also an integral part of the site, which the new visitor centre at Abbotsford, built in 2013, serves. The site, which slopes down to the river, upon which it borders, is noteworthy for its abundance of trees (Scott started planting trees on the site before he even took possession of the land, and went on to design and lay out the estate himself) and for being home to wildlife such as deer and red squirrels.

The siting of Abbotsford visitor centre was a challenging one and addresses a problem common to many visitor centres. First, you want the visitor centre and reception/welcome desk (particularly if access is controlled and tickets need to be purchased) to be as close to the car park as possible. Second, you equally want visitors to be able to view the attraction upon arrival and immediately orient themselves; if the visitor centre sits between the car park and the attraction (as it does in the case of Abbotsford) then the visitor centre will, most likely, block any welcoming views of the attraction. In the case of the Abbotsford visitor centre, the house can scarcely be seen upon arrival; rather it is the visitor centre that initially visually dominates any first impressions of the site.

The entrance to the permanent exhibition area of Abbotsford's visitor centre

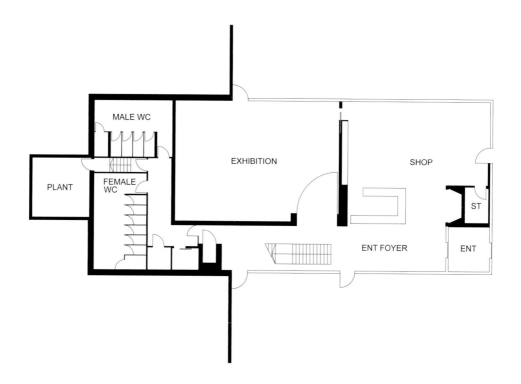

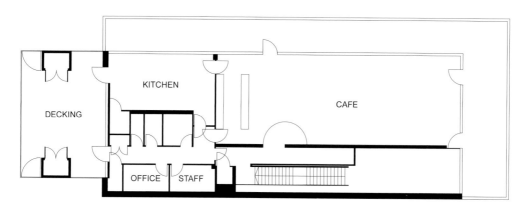

0   10m

N

Plans of Abbotsford

top: View from the first-floor balcony/walkway looking towards the roofs of Abbotsford House (the inner side of the balustrade, is inscribed with a quotation of Scott)

above: The first-floor restaurant terrace of Abbotsford visitor centre

Upon closer inspection, the siting and orientation of the visitor centre is quite perceptive. The visitor centre is a relatively long, thin building that is positioned perpendicular to the direction of movement into the site (and hence towards the house), with its entrance located on its short façade and, as such, it does not really appear to be oriented towards Abbotsford House at all, rather its relationship seems, at first glance, to be oriented towards the River Tweed. In fact, the relationship between the two buildings has been very carefully considered. Having its longest façade facing towards the house provides the greatest expanse of views towards the house (from the interior of the visitor centre). The positioning of its entrance also permits a brief, tantalising glimpse of Abbotsford House: you arrive at the visitor centre, not 'frontally' but 'edge-on', so that at the point of arrival you are positioned to look directly past the visitor centre towards an enticing view of the house's rooftops in the distance beyond. Furthermore, at the entrance to the visitor centre, the roof sails over the path, forming a large canopy that is supported by two, incredibly slender, wooden columns. This configuration of roof canopy and columns serves to frame these views of Abbotsford's roofs in the far distance and so, before turning to enter the visitor centre, the visitor is simultaneously oriented on site and their destination laid out before them in the landscape.

The massing of the visitor centre is intriguing as it is a two-storey building that, somehow, feels 'low slung'; it is as if it is holding on to the landscape rather than floating above it and hence it feels very 'grounded' as a building. It is unashamedly modernist in style, clean and minimal, and yet surprisingly, the predominant material is timber (perhaps not an inappropriate choice for an estate where tree-planting had been almost an obsession); it is a building that owes far more to the concrete Modernism of the early twentieth century than to the vernacular styles that the wooden cladding suggests. As is typical with wooden cladding, the wood has weathered and now has taken on a slightly silvered, slightly mottled appearance that seems to help camouflage it amid the trees that grow all around, and surprisingly close to, the building.

Formally, the building is a long thin box, with the second storey accommodating a wrap-around balcony (oriented towards the house) which forms a generous balcony/terrace (used as an outdoor cafe space) above the entrance, over which sails a dramatic canopy roof. The portal frame structure of the building is clearly articulated inside as a series of wooden frames stepping back through the building, and therefore the diagram is one where, in the horizontal plane, the rhythm of the building is dictated by the regular spacing of these portal frames. Vertically, the building is read as having three distinct layers: the ground floor which is mostly glazed; the second floor appearing fully clad (the windows are set back behind the balcony, so what you 'read' as being façade is really the edge of the balcony and the third element, the oversized canopy roof. This interplay of the regular horizontal frames and the vertical banding of glass, wood cladding and roof appear like the warp and weft of some woven fabric, perhaps even a tartan.

Upon entering the building you find yourself in a bright, double-height space and are immediately faced by the welcome desk, to your right, and stairs leading to the first-floor restaurant. The shop is immediately behind the welcome desk and further into the depth of the building, on the ground floor, is an exhibition area devoted to the life of Sir Walter Scott and Abbotsford House. The museum exhibition follows a single route terminating in a well-lit room, facing towards the House, in which there is also a model of the house. This is the pinnacle of the experience: while scrutinising the model, beyond it, in the distance; you are rewarded with the first full view of the house, framed through the window with its model displayed before it. The best views of the house, however, are from the first-floor restaurant's windows and from the cafe's balcony at the end of the building. From these higher vantage points, the overall composition and massing of the house is revealed. There is a clear intention that this location should be used to view the building since, on the inner side of the balustrade, is inscribed a quotation, 'My heart clings to the place I have created', this well-chosen quote encapsulates the spirit of this place.

Alnwick Gardens

FULL NAME

Alnwick Garden Pavilion and Visitor Centre

ARCHITECTS

Hopkins Architects

COMPLETION DATE

2006

COST

£7,200,000

COST/m²

£3,600

NEAREST POSTCODE

NE66 1YU

SELECTED AWARDS

RIBA Regional Award 2008

Structural Steel Design Award 2007

The Wood Awards – Highly Commended 2006

Garden
Water

top: Roof structure of Alnwick Garden
Pavilion showing part of the inflated
transparent and translucent 'pillows'

above: Alnwick Garden Pavilion viewed from
the steps alongside the 'Grand Cascade'
(the garden's stepped water feature)

The approach to Alnwick Garden Visitor Centre and Pavilion is gently uphill, following a generous path leading from the main car park to the buildings, and is lined with hedges on either side, so that the Visitor Centre remains hidden from view for most of the ascent. The first glimpse afforded to the visitor is of an arched, glass gable of the building in which the admissions entry-space is located. This view, obtained over the tops of the hedges, gives away little about the somewhat quirky nature of the building, other than the fact that arched curves play a strong formal role.

This is a visitor centre in two parts and hence reveals itself only incrementally. Unknown to the first-time visitor, this initial view is of just one part (and the minor part at that) of the assemblage of buildings. As the visitor draws closer to the admissions space, they might become aware of the unusual roofline, as they are presented with a side-view of one of the two wings of the visitor centre building (which is approximately U-shaped, forming a courtyard space: this wing being one of the arms of the U-shape). The roofline is unusual; constructed with inflated transparent and translucent 'pillows', held in place by a regular, curved timber lattice-shell.

On the one hand, the plastic, inflated 'hillocks' of the roof are as far removed from anything botanical, as it is possible to get. If anything 'natural' is brought to mind it is more along the lines of perfectly aligned frogspawn (minus the black 'dot' in the middle), but there is also something suggestive in the impeccably white and gentle curves of the cotton boll (the white protective case around its seeds) to the roof lines. But it is clear that the intention is to create a modern greenhouse, and that the use of the inflated roof-cells are functional, they provide insulation from the cold as well as reducing overheating in the summer. And since glasshouses were

unabashedly modern when they first came into use, there is no reason why this modern interpretation of the traditional greenhouse should feel out of place in a garden. These inflatable 'panes' are nothing more than the traditional glasshouse panes given a rather cheeky, modern, bubbly spin.

Once through the admissions space, the visitor will probably pass through the shop to emerge into the courtyard formed by the two wings of this first building. This is where the building's full material palette and architectural language are revealed. From the courtyard, the language of the barrel-vaults, the wooden lattice-grid and inflatable cellular roofs, wooden, tree-like columns, sprouting tapering, branched-struts, is evident. What is also tentatively revealed is the nature of the building/s as being in two halves: what divides the two parts of the building is a solid, impressively high, stone wall. This is the garden wall of the original eighteenth-century garden. And the wall is not an incidental component of the building/s, rather it is critical to the siting and design of the two halves, playing a different role for each half. On the shop/admissions side, the wall serves to form the fourth and completing wall of the courtyard. Three sides of the courtyard are created by the U-shape of the new building, and the fourth is the impressive, monumental stone garden wall (albeit a wall that does not 'touch' the new building making the courtyard-space 'porous').

As the unfamiliar, first-time visitor emerges from the shop, they will probably realise that they are now positioned on axis to the only visible feature in this massive wall, an equally generous and gated archway. This is strongly evocative of the archetypal 'secret garden' of literature, the garden hidden behind the wall, yielding its mysteries and surprises only to the select few (in this case, the

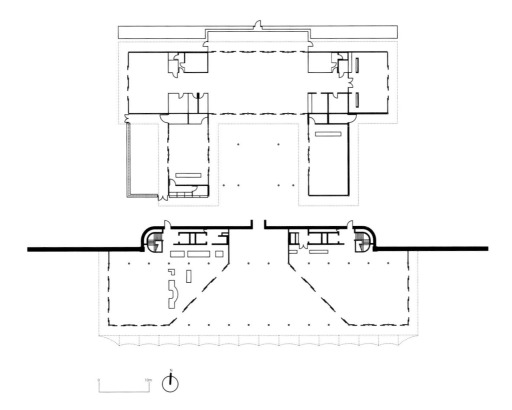

Plan of Alnwick Gardens

top: Alnwick Gardens' partial 'courtyard' looking towards the shop

above: The Alnwick Garden, main visitor entrance

ticket-holders); the entrance to the shop is precisely aligned to this iconic archway to the garden, each located on opposite sides of the courtyard: this is a highly formal and symmetrical building. Through the archway, further tantalising glimpses can be had of more of the same architectural language of lattice roof, white billowing, inflatable 'pillows' and wooden columns, in the foreground, and, in the distance, the formal cascade of water, for which Alnwick has become well known since its recent redevelopment.

Once through the archway, the role that the original garden wall plays in the other part of the building, the Pavilion, is revealed. For this half of the building, rather than holding the garden wall 'at a distance' as the courtyard building does, this building embraces it, using the wall as one of its exterior walls, and so incorporating it fully into the building, as a fusion of old and new. This building is a single, 64m long, barrel-vaulted, single-storey building. It is symmetrical about the original archway, which perforates the wall mid-way along one of the long sides of the building. The roof continues, without interruption, along the building's length, altering only in terms of its translucency (more transparent in the central section). In the middle part, the roof is merely a canopy, for the space immediately in front of the archway is an exterior space, a terrace overlooking the garden, which is laid out in front of it. This exterior space is funnel-shaped in plan, maximising these initial views to the garden. From the moment of passing through the archway (the symbolic entering of the 'secret garden') all is revealed in an instant, the visitor has to wait no longer, and this is enabled by the splayed walls of the rooms either side of the terrace. One of these spaces is the cafe (with kitchens and other auxiliary spaces located below ground) and the other is a flexible space, a

multi-function room. The terrace however, occupies approximately the same floor area as these two rooms, and so the long building is effectively divided into three, by the funnel-shaped terrace. Given how much space is dedicated to something that is effectively a 'non-space', a functionless space, this shows how important this sense of arrival – of being able to instantaneously appraise and appreciate the afforded views – is to the scheme. This experience of passing through the archway and then instantly arriving 'somewhere else' is part of the magic of the garden and it is this transition from the everyday to the 'extraordinary' that is afforded by the planning and composition of the building.

Finally, the key fact about vistas is that just as a view can be seen from a single standpoint, this relationship is reciprocal; hence, from the garden, the views to the pavilion are equally impressive. In particular, if a visitor takes the time to climb the steps alongside the 'Grand Cascade' (the garden's stepped water feature), framed views of the pavilion can be seen through arched 'windows' in the curved pergolas that follow the edges of the 'Grand Cascade'. Finally, from the top of the cascade, the pavilion is laid out below, resembling the traditional glasshouses or orangeries of previous generations of gardeners. The architects have managed quite a feat in their modern interpretation of a traditional garden building.

Bannockburn

KEY FACTS

FULL NAME

Bannockburn Battlefield Visitor Centre

ARCHITECTS

Reiach and Hall Architects

COMPLETION DATE

2014

COST

£9,100,000

COST/m²

£7,022

NEAREST POSTCODE

FK7 0LL

SELECTED AWARDS

RICS Tourism and Leisure Project of the Year Award 2015

European Union Prize for Contemporary Architecture – Mies van der Rohe Award – Nominated 2015

Civic Trust Awards – Commendation 2015

Scottish Property Awards Architectural Excellence – Highly Commended 2015

Scottish Design Awards Architecture Grand Prix 2014

Scottish Design Awards Leisure/Cultural Building of the Year 2014

Battle,
History
Nationalism

Main entrance to Bannockburn

It goes without saying that a visitor centre is, for the most part, sited precisely where it needs to be sited and, in the case of a famous battle, this might not correspond to any modern logic as to where a visitor centre should be sited. It might be out in the middle of nowhere, in a field or on the moors, such as it is at Culloden, or it might be in the middle of a modern-day settlement, such as Bannockburn. It is for this reason that when arriving at Bannockburn Visitor Centre, it feels like a little bit of a surprise. The building is set back from the road, and has residential buildings, a hotel and a school as neighbours and so the setting seems somewhat commonplace, rather than extraordinary. Of course, this is real challenge for a visitor centre such as Bannockburn. It exists because of something that happened a long time ago, in the same place, but where there are no traces in the landscape to identify this site as being different from any other location. So how do architects and visitor centre designers design something that elevates the commonplace to the 'exceptional place' (Relph) and, at the same time, to render the invisible, visible? To help reach back in time to when the location was significant?

In actual fact, the site at Bannockburn was not completely devoid of any traces or references to the battle, there already existed a monument (1870s flagpole and 1960s rotunda and Robert the Bruce statue). The architects' tasks regarding the new visitor centre were to rationalise the site, integrate parking, views and access to the monument while providing all of the facilities and interpretive exhibits expected of a modern visitor centre. The first thing that the visitor to this building needs to understand is that the alignment on site is paramount. The irregular six-sided building is not simply a wilful play on the aesthetics of irregularity, rather it is an attempt to visually connect the monument to the car park, which in turn has to relate to the street, while also relating in scale and orientation to the neighbouring buildings, many of which were domestic. The resultant form is essentially an irregular polygon, with tall, relatively featureless walls, around an irregular courtyard. Within the mass of the polygonal footprint is contained a rotunda space – the heart of the interpretive exhibition. There is

also a shift in scale between the outside and the inside, whereas the outside is two stories in height, the courtyard is only single-storey, with the roofs angled down towards the centre of the building. Equally, while the exterior of the building comprises of rather austere, muted façades made of engineering brick, the interior of the courtyard is predominately white, oriented to the sky and hence rather uplifting. This contrast between exterior-exterior and courtyard-exterior is quite striking and contributes to the sense that this is a somewhat private, introspective building.

Given that this is one of the few visitor centres featured in this book that commemorates a battle, it also begs the question, how does one remember and represent something that resulted in such great loss of life? The statistics at Bannockburn are astounding: the number of Scottish dead was held to be low in contrast to the English casualties, which possibly numbered around 11,000. We clearly cannot say that such a visitor centre 'celebrates' the battle, as this would be wrong, so how can a building portray the correct degree of respect and consideration for the dead, without being, in turn, an unpleasant place to be in? The nature of this contradiction – designing a place that is enjoyable to visit while being respectful of the dead – goes some way to explaining the intriguing introspective and contemplative character of the building.

As you approach from the car park, the building is set back and appears smaller than expected. The nature of its irregular polygonal footprint means that only the front façade is visible from the street, no other elevations can be seen. The front façade contains the only large expanse, floor to roof, of glazing; this is the double-height, out-facing shop and entrance space. As mentioned above, the use of brick in this building is particularly noteworthy. First, the architects used a dark engineering brick that, particularly in wet weather (not uncommon in Scotland), can vary from a mid-grey to an almost black appearance. Although the overall effect is quite sombre, as mentioned above, the relentlessness of the façade is relieved through variations in the brick bonds used. Some sections are English bond; others Flemish and others have

top: Main façade and shop windows to Bannockburn

above: Roof space and lighting above the shop at Bannockburn

alternating bricks recessed to give a chequerboard effect. Overall, this manages to alleviate what would otherwise be a set of somewhat dour and austere elevations and provides points of interest and focus for the eye.

Upon entering the building, the contrast between the dark bulk of the exterior and the lightness of touch of the interior is quite marked. The material palette inside is predominantly untreated, pale timber and white-painted steel, with views to, and across, the courtyard from almost all sides. The only other elevation that has a strong visual relationship to the outside is the cafe at the rear of the building, which looks out over the battlefield and towards the monument. These views are facilitated via a ribbon of single-storey glass at ground-floor level. Aside from these two expanses of glass, all other openings in the exterior of the building are kept to a minimum; some façades are without any openings at all, and where necessary they are accommodated by small, almost square, mullion-less windows, which appear to become part of the varying chequerboard patterns of the bricks.

Of all the things that the building appears to resemble, with its dearth of openings and minimal windows, it is a medieval castle or fortified house,

turning inward to protect itself from attack. Given that the Battle of Bannockburn was fought in 1314, at a time when castles were still being built, this analogy is perhaps not accidental, and as such, manages to capture not only something of the place, but perhaps also something of the time that it commemorates.

No review of this building would be complete without mention of the interior rotunda and interpretive exhibitions. The rotunda houses a raked theatre of a size and scale not dissimilar to early dissecting 'theatres' for the training of medical students. In the centre of the space, rather than a corpse, there is instead a table upon which a digital battle-simulation can be enacted. The cutting-edge use of digital technologies (although not strictly part of the architectural language of the building, nevertheless has an impact of the design and layout of it) is one of the most remarkable surprises to be found within the building. This is the closest that visitors can come to experiencing what it would have been like to be on the battlefield all those centuries ago. The design of the digital exhibits has not been an afterthought, but was clearly designed to be integral to the building (and vice versa) and as such they work together synergistically.

Bannockburn's northern façade

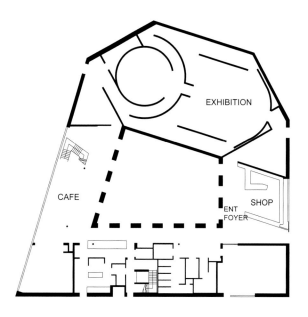

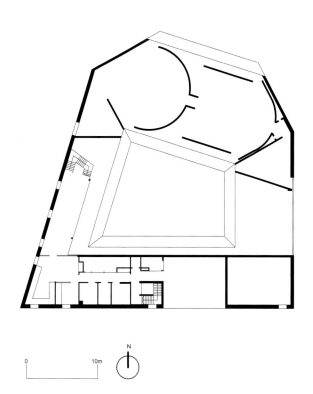

Plans of Bannockburn

Bombay Sapphire

KEY FACTS

FULL NAME
Bombay Sapphire Distillery Visitor Centre

ARCHITECTS
Heatherwick Studio

COMPLETION DATE
2014

COST
Unavailable

COST/m²
Unavailable

NEAREST POSTCODE
RG28 7NR

SELECTED AWARDS
***Architect's Journal* Annual Retrofit Award – Shortlisted 2016**
BREEAM Industrial Award 2014

Commercial
Industrial
History
Reuse

Bombay Sapphire's botanical glasshouses

**Views along the River Test showing a
glimpse of the botanical glasshouses above
the roofs**

The Bombay Sapphire Visitor Centre makes a particularly interesting visitor centre case study for a number of reasons: first, it is one of the very few examples in the book where the 'attraction' at the heart of the visitor centre experience is an everyday place of work for a sizeable workforce: the Bombay Sapphire Distillery Visitor Centre is also the working distillery of the Bombay Sapphire Gin Company; second, it is also of interest as it is an example of where the designer (Thomas Heatherwick) had already built up a long-standing relationship with the client (ten years earlier Heatherwick had won the inaugural Bombay Sapphire Prize for innovation in glass), and was then invited back to not only to provide the master plan for the distillery site (when it was being transformed from an disused Victorian paper (banknote) mill into a modern gin distillery), but also to provide visitor centre facilities alongside his master planning endeavour; and finally, it is a particularly interesting example of the creative reuse of a former historical mill with the addition of some tightly focused, new-build interventions.

As mentioned above, the site of the distillery was a former eighteenth to nineteenth century paper/banknote mill located in the village of Laverstoke in Hampshire (although there had been a mill of some description on the site since, at least 1086). The vast majority of the buildings on the site date back to the mid-eighteenth century and the site was initially purchased by Bombay Sapphire in 2010. Heatherwick Studio's master planning exercise required, first and foremost, the rationalisation of the higgledy accretion of buildings that had gradually accumulated to cover most of the site (of the 49 original buildings on the site, approximately half needed to be removed as part of this rationalisation process). One goal behind this reduction and removal of buildings was to re-reveal the River Test, the river flowing through the site, as both the raison d'être for, as well as a central feature of, the site. Another goal was to create a balance between the needs of the workforce and the visitors' experience (and finally to do so in a manner not only respectful of the historic environment, but also sustainable).

On arrival at the village of Laverstoke, you are struck by the disparities of scale between the village and the distillery, since the latter dominates the former. The visitor will typically arrive at the car park and upon entering the site, be taken immediately to its heart, namely the River Test, running directly through the middle of the site. From the vantage point of the first of two footbridges spanning the river, the red brick industrial buildings are displayed to their best advantage against the vivid green of the lush grasses and reeds that have now been permitted, even encouraged, to flourish alongside the banks of the Test. The buildings, organised around the river, are classic examples of the best of eighteenth/nineteenth-century brick industrial buildings. The scale of these buildings is quite intimate, as they seem to huddle around the river's banks and, along with the verdant greenery of the reeds, this renders it an oasis of calm. And yet, already, all is not what it seems, for from the footbridge's vantage point a glimpse of something rather alien in the landscape, emerging from between the roofs of two of the staid Victorian buildings, can be spotted: an interloper, a 'Triffid' lurking amid the local fauna. Yet, on approaching the entrance, this glimpse of the bizarre recedes again, almost as if it were a dream.

Parts of the visitor centre are accommodated in these former buildings, the shop, the bar (for the all-important gin tasting) and the reception area, where the tour begins. The style of these

Bombay Sapphire, showing the relationship
between the botanical glasshouses and the
existing buildings

**Bombay Sapphire, showing some of the
original Victorian buildings framed by the
botanical glasshouses**

refurbishments are very much that of the clean, minimal, stripped back New York loft-style, transplanted into rural Hampshire; in other words, the epitome of the trendy, industrial shabby-chic aesthetic. Once through the reception, the visitor emerges once more into a sheltered courtyard surrounded by more red brick buildings, it is a pleasant, humanly-scaled open space, formed by buildings on three sides and an open lawn on the fourth side. But this sense of cosy containment is turned upside-down as the visitor is suddenly confronted by what lies beyond the lawn. What Heatherwick Studio have created here almost defies description, for a pair of entwined, flower-trumpet protuberances are bursting, alien-like from an existing vernacular building (rather like the alien exploding from the crewman's chest in the movie of the same name and equally as shocking). It would not surprise me if the majority of visitors are stuck motionless in surprise upon first seeing these; they are as joyful, playful and exuberant as they are unexpected.

These protuberances are in fact, botanical glass-houses, designed to showcase living examples of the ten botanicals (juniper, lemon peel, grains of paradise, coriander, cubeb berries, orris root, almonds, cassia bark, liquorice, angelica) that contribute to the distinctive taste of Bombay Sapphire gin. One glasshouse houses tropical, and the other temperate, plants. Each glasshouse is, in plan, a sixteen-sided star, but with very shallow points, rather more like a crinkled cookie cutter than a star. These sixteen star-points effectively make 32 alternatively angled glazed panels that initially are extruded vertically, before suddenly curving and twisting into their individual funnel-shapes, one 15m high, the other 11m. In total, the two glasshouses contain 793 curved glass sections. Formally, they are reminiscent not only of Victorian glasshouses (Paxton's

magnificent Crystal Palace immediately comes to mind) but equally, at the same time, there is also something rather evocative in the iconic, curvy, copper gin stills. Indeed, inside the building (from which the glasshouses appear to burst) are two such examples of historic copper gin stills, and despite the differences in scale and materiality, the formal similarities are discernible. Other formal comparisons that can be made with the glasshouses are giant gin bottles and analogies to the sinuous, blossoming, lush botanicals themselves. Another poetic aspect of the glasshouses is that their faceted, glass exteriors reflect the historic buildings around them, so that the old and new are fused into an irregular collage of the two. The relationship between the glasshouses and the building to which it is joined is not just a formal one. The glasshouses are literally funnels through which the warm, waste heat of the distillation process is pumped from the still house in order to heat the glasshouses. And so the relationship of the new to the old is not just formal, but literally symbiotic, since the glasshouses rely on this waste heat to function. In addition to the poetic elegance of the glasshouses, this was the first distillery and first refurbishment to achieve an 'Outstanding' design-stage BREEAM (Building Research Establishment's Environmental Assessment Method) accreditation.

There is no question that this overall scheme represents an exceptional transformation of an old, derelict and chaotic site into something quite magical. The rationalisation and reuse of the historic buildings, the revealing and reinstatement of the river, and the joyful, exuberant, luscious glasshouses are a tour de force. Heatherwick Studio has not only managed to create an inspiring new workplace, but a visitor experience unlike any other.

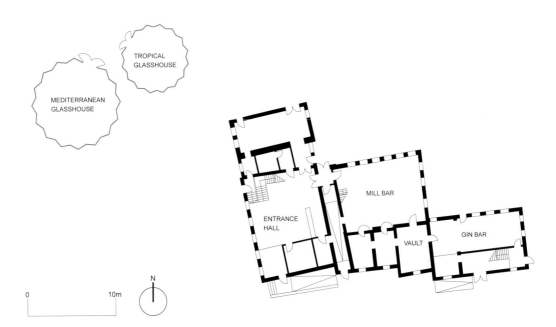

TROPICAL
GLASSHOUSE

MEDITERRANEAN
GLASSHOUSE

MILL BAR

ENTRANCE
HALL

VAULT

GIN BAR

0   10m

N

Plan of Bombay Sapphire

Brockholes

FULL NAME

Brockholes Wetland and Woodland Nature Reserve

ARCHITECTS

Adam Khan Architects

COMPLETION DATE

2011

COST

£6,250,000

COST/m²

£4,464

NEAREST POSTCODE

PR5 0AG

SELECTED AWARDS

RIBA National Award 2012

Stirling Prize mid-list 2012

Civic Trust Award 2012

Civic Trust Special Award for Sustainability 2012

Wood Awards 2011 – Winner

BREEAM 'Outstanding'

Wildlife
Wetland
Water
Floating

top: Brockholes floating on the lake
amongst the reeds

above: Brockholes, showing one of the
floating paths and drawbridges in the
distance

top: Reflections in the ceiling above the
restaurant/cafe in Brockholes

above: Brockholes, showing textures of the
hand-cut, oak shingles

Brockholes is, unlike many other visitor centres, located in both a convenient yet somewhat inauspicious location: in this case, directly off Junction 31 of the M6. Having negotiated motorway slip roads, no less than three roundabouts, and a bridge over the River Ribble, you eventually find yourself on the right path to Brockholes Nature Reserve (or the 'unreserved reserve' as its sign proudly proclaims), a reclaimed wetland habitat owned by The Lancashire Wildlife Trust.

At first, the approach seems quite drawn-out, an unremarkable road flanked by unremarkable scrub-trees when suddenly, to your right, the Meadow Lake and its visitor centre appears, in all of its striking middle-of-the-lake-ness, entirety – looking, as much as anything, like an Iron-Age village. All of a sudden, and at once, there it is: as if to give you a tantalising glimpse of what is yet to come. It is reminiscent of a testing method used to evaluate websites in which the user is presented with a webpage for exactly five seconds, the image removed and the user is asked what they remember seeing. Given that this initial glimpse of the visitor centre is almost exactly five seconds long (if speeding past in a car) this analogy is very apt. What did you see? What did you remember? What was your first impression?

When approaching it for the second time, the visitor is on foot and this time the appearance of the building is more gradual and far subtler. The visitor approaches indirectly, following a curved path; the visitor centre is initially hidden from view by the landscape and as you come nearer it is gradually revealed in a smooth transition.

As mentioned above, this is a visitor centre ('building' is certainly a misnomer as it is really a set of buildings, a complex, perhaps even a 'visitor village' as the Nature Reserve terms it) set in the middle of a lake and accessed via floating paths, drawbridges, and portcullises. It is hard to describe the sheer visceral excitement of a floating building: it immediately brings to mind medieval castles protected by moats (and yet this is the exact opposite of defensive architecture as it is designed to welcome not repel, and without doubt it welcomes by inviting further exploration). But this is where the analogy with the castle and the moat is simultaneously apt yet misleading. A castle clearly does not float, it is solidly set into the ground and the moat merely encircles it, and yet this building most emphatically does float (it is built onto a pontoon, engineered by Price & Myers and Max Fordham, constructed of a cellular reinforced concrete structure with polystyrene infills). One of the first impressions of the building is of its hulking mass (this is where the analogy with the castle is apt) and yet this mass of building appears to defy intuitive logic by floating. The contrast between heaviness and lightness plays games with your mind and is testament to both the design and engineering that this trick of playing with such contradictions is pulled off so deftly.

Once you have stepped onto the pontoon, the impression formed from afar is confirmed, that this is a building (or set of buildings) that is all about 'the roof'. For most buildings, roofs are little more than a functional necessity, often more of a design afterthought than a design feature and are frequently hidden from view as if concealing something to be embarrassed about. But this building exuberantly celebrates its roof: indeed the whole design could be said to be about the roof, the roofline, its profile and texture: the hipped roofs seemingly point every which way in an almost fractal manner, with the smaller roofs being mathematically similar versions of their larger siblings. Another iconic feature of the Brockholes' roofs, which also draws attention to them and renders them instantly recognisable in images and photographs, are the random assortment of shiny, mirror-finish vents perched on top: a shininess that contrasts pleasantly with the roofs' hand-cut, oak shingles. This is a visitor centre about water, reeds, glass and roofs but most importantly about textures. And, like many buildings next to water or with water features, when the sun is shining the light reflects off the water and plays on the different surfaces of the buildings, providing an additional, layering of textures, but this time dynamic ones.

The roofs' dominance continues as the visitor moves inside the buildings, for the roof volumes are unusually large and open to the spaces below. In most of the interior spaces, the geometry of the roof-beams forms intriguing patterns above the visitors' heads, while the ceiling above the cafe's serving counter is clad in highly reflective stainless steel creating surreal and distorted reflections of the visitors' heads while queuing for food and so the eye is drawn ever upwards. (The overall impression of the cafe space is extremely pleasant as there really is nothing quite like eating while looking out over water).

Although this is a building (or set of buildings) that clearly wants to be looked at, it is far subtler when it comes to views *around*, and views *from*, the buildings than first impressions might suggest. First, moving around the pontoon, either inside or outside the buildings, causes sudden vistas (particularly those looking out over the lake) to be momentarily revealed. Then, when inside, the visitor finds that windows are located in unexpected places, so that a quick reminder of the watery landscape beyond is shown, and then disappears just as suddenly. The clustering of the buildings around the external 'courtyards' in the middle of the pontoon, also means that when looking out of any individual

building on the pontoon, you can find yourself looking from the inside-to-the-outside and then as your gaze passes beyond that, from the outside-to-the-inside again, and then once more to the outside. The result is a complex layering effect of views that makes the visual experience feel far richer than it might otherwise be. This effect is either the result of a merely unforeseen consequence of the placement of the buildings (a happy accident), or is indicative of a very adroit architectural hand.

In consequence, it is very hard not to like this building (or pontoon, or floating village …) enormously: first it really is, simply, rather fun (and perhaps we do not sufficiently celebrate this aspect of architecture as much as we should), second the experience of walking around it is a constant feast for the senses with its emphasis on repetitive, fractal-like forms and strong textures and finally, it cannot be accused of being inauthentic and of not responding to the context of the site, since the site is a completely man-made, reclaimed environment. The landscape that we see at Brockholes today does not reflect any past landscape, it is entirely new and made-up and therefore why not also add to this landscape a whimsical, floating Iron-Age(ish) village, which would not have existed here either? The building and the landscape are equally true to each other, as each has been creatively reinvented and reimagined, where before there was nothing remarkable.

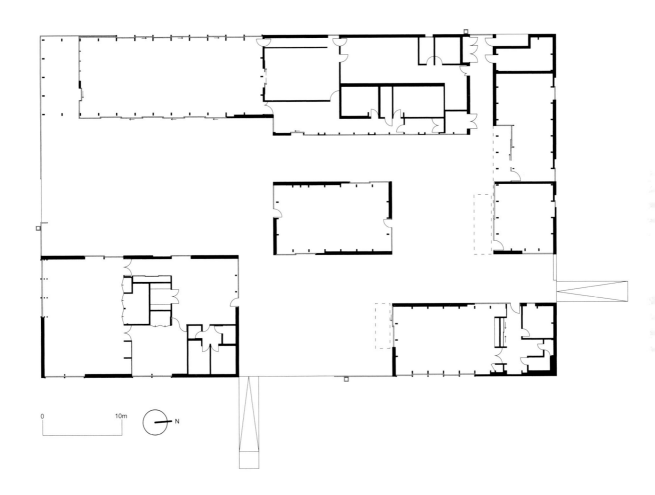

0   10m   N

Plan of Brockholes

Chedworth Roman Villa

KEY FACTS

FULL NAME

Chedworth Roman Villa

ARCHITECTS

Feilden Clegg Bradley Studios

COMPLETION DATE

2012

COST

£2,000,000

COST/m²

£4,348

NEAREST POSTCODE

GL54 3LJ

SELECTED AWARDS

RIBA National Award 2013

CPRE Gloucestershire Awards 2012

top: Chedworth Roman Villa showing the
suspended walkways

above: Interior of Chedworth Roman Villa,
looking along the ambulatory (corridor) towards
the main entrance, taken from the exit

The approach to Chedworth Roman Villa, situated in an Area of Outstanding Natural Beauty in the middle of the Cotswolds, feels as if you are heading into the middle of nowhere, as the roads become ever more narrow and more 'rural' (how far from the centre of Rome must this have felt when it was built?). Eventually a small and modest signpost saying, simply, 'Roman Villa' reassures you that you are not utterly lost. Nevertheless, the site feels curiously secluded and removed from the everyday world. Trees surround it on three sides and on the fourth there are open views across the countryside to the River Coln. In the Victorian age, and immediately prior to this, these woods would have entirely covered the site: the trees immediately surrounding the villa were only cleared after its accidental discovery by a gamekeeper in 1864, hence the feeling of being tightly enclosed by the wood. The site, once uncovered, turned out to be one of the most significant Roman archaeological sites in England; the complex of buildings formed a country estate that was inhabited for approximately 250 years from the second century AD and included a water shrine, hypocausts (clearly visible today), bath houses, walls and many, lavish mosaics. The National Trust acquired the property in 1924 and decided to ensure the future preservation of the remains, particularly the mosaics, via a new protective 'shelter' as well as to rationalise the entire visitor experience by providing more up-to-date and flexible facilities.

If we consider the spatial relationship between the visitor centre and the 'attraction', (explored in Chapter 1) Chedworth Roman Villa is particularly fascinating, as the visitor centre is, to all intents and purposes, 'on top of' its attraction. The new building sits on top of the original Roman foundations of the western wing of the complex (known as the West Range). The most visible remains today

form three sides (the North and South Ranges are the other two) around a, now grassy, courtyard. The fourth side, directly opposite the West Range, is the site of a Victorian building, which was built after the discovery of the villa. The challenge of how to build on top of a delicate, archaeological site, without causing any damage to the existing remains, yet also providing it with protection from the weather in a controlled environment, was one of the architectural challenges of this scheme. The solution is that the new timber structure was designed to be as lightweight as possible and is self-supporting: it does not need to be fixed to the Roman foundations nor walls. What is particularly ingenious about this method of construction is that due to this, literally, 'light touch' approach the new structure could, at some point in the future, be reconfigured or entirely removed if required.

Formally, the timber structure consists of an asymmetrically pitched roof (steeper at the front; shallower to the rear) section extruded, prism-like, along the length of the building, terminating abruptly with flat gables at either end. This extruded form is then articulated by the regular rhythm of larch timber cladding (grown on the National Trust's estate at Ashridge in Hertfordshire), formed by a series of carefully spaced, vertical batons. These batons start at ground level and, once they meet the eaves of the roof, are then picked up again as cladding for the roof. Where there are windows, these are concealed behind the relentless, marching regularity of the batons, which also serve the functional purpose of reducing solar gain and hence preventing the sun from damaging the mosaic floors inside. The overall effect of this is as if the extruded form of the building has simply been 'wrapped' or draped in the larch batons. This lack of any other formal gesture – simply the minimal form placed over the

top: Main façade of Chedworth Roman
Villa showing larch cladding

above: Main façade of Chedworth Roman
Villa, looking towards the exit

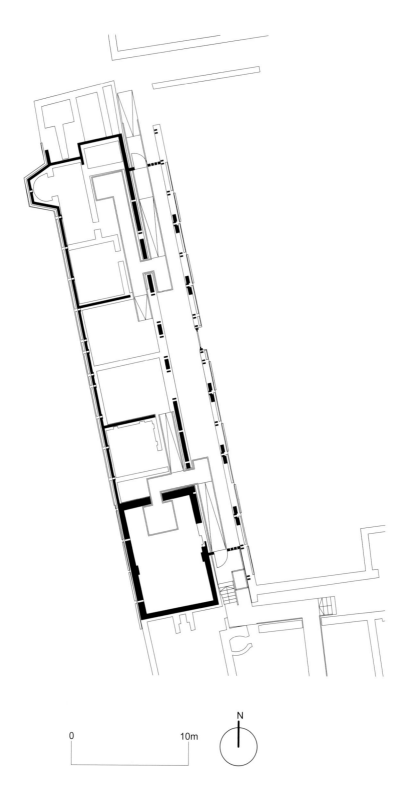

Plan of Chedworth Roman Villa

remains – does not give any hint to the visitor of how the Roman villa might have appeared. It would have been very tempting to try to reconstruct, if not the appearance, then at the very least the composition and massing of the original building, but it is clear at first glance that this is no attempt at a reconstruction. The architects have chosen to contrast the old with the new: materially, formally and spatially. The simplicity and clarity of the building also contrasts with the rather higgledy irregularity of the archaeological remains. Finally, the use of the larch cladding reflects the building's rural setting and the fact that for hundreds of years, trees grew through the remains of the building, until it had become entirely incorporated into forest. Although cleared by the Victorians, the wood has returned, but this time in a controlled and protective way, rather than a destructive one.

Once inside the building, the visitor is gradually raised above the original floor level by a series of metal walkways that appear to float over the mosaic floors, permitting the visitor to gaze directly down upon the intricate patterns of the mosaics. These walkways are ramped at either end of the building, permitting a more inclusive access than would have been available in the past. In the centre of the building, the architects have created a new Interpretation Room, which can be used for exhibition purposes and as a flexible education space. The sequence of spaces in the building is very symmetrical: first the walkway ramps up and you view the mosaics of the former dining room of the villa, then you emerge into the generous, open space of the Interpretation Room, next you move deeper into the building to view the Bath House mosaics and finally the walkway ramps down again to ground level. And thus your experience of leaving the building is a direct reflection of your experience of entering: it feels balanced and harmonious.

These walkways, like the timber structure, are equally lightweight and are suspended from beams in the ceiling. The careful detailing and clear, white walls, ensure that the Roman building is always the centre of attention. The effect is similar to the classic 'white cube' art gallery where the patron is meant only to attend to the art but in this case the 'art' is the archaeology. Let us revisit the primary objective of this building: the architects said that they 'wanted the Roman archaeology to take centre stage'. In Chapter 2, the question was posed of how can architects design for 'exceptional settings' and one of the ways suggested was by making the building 'invisible'. In many respects this building is the epitome of that approach, and is proudly proclaimed as such by the architects. In this chapter the corollary was also discussed, that by doing so, the architects run the risk of designing a building that is bland and uninspiring and so the question must be asked, is this a bland building? The suggestion is that it is not, and the secret behind this is the fact that the attraction and the building are coincident and so the visitors' attention is always focused on the Roman building, not the new one. Here we have an example of the architects willingly subsuming their own egos to a higher purpose.

Chiltern Hills Gateway

KEY FACTS

FULL NAME

Chiltern Hills Gateway

ARCHITECTS

Architype

COMPLETION DATE

2007

COST

£2,500,000

COST/m²

£4,132

NEAREST POSTCODE

LU6 2GY

SELECTED AWARDS

Sustainable Building of the Year – Finalist 2007

Geology
Landscape
Wind

Chiltern Hills Gateway looking down the main façade
towards the chalk escarpment

top: Chiltern Hills Gateway showing the
relationship between the building and the
landscape beyond

above: Chiltern Hills Gateway's main
façade and external sitting area

While not being located in the most inhospitable of places (since that accolade must surely go to the Hafod Eryri visitor centre on the top of Snowdon mountain) the Chiltern Hills Gateway visitor centre, set atop a steep, chalk escarpment (namely an inland, natural geological outcrop with a gentle slope on one side and a far steeper slope on the other) in the Chiltern Downs, is certainly located in one of the windiest of locations in England. It can therefore be suggested that wind and views to the landscape (the site of the visitor centre commands the most outstanding views across the Vale of Aylesbury) are the raisons d'être of this building.

The Dunstable and Whipsnade Downs are, without question, a beautiful landscape on the edge of the steep chalk escarpment and the area is also a Site of Special Scientific Interest (SSSI) due to the chalk grassland species found there. (In addition to this, the Icknield Way, considered the 'oldest road in Britain', also follows the line of the escarpment ridge, and hence passes very close to the visitor centre.) The chalk downs are, even for a non-geologist, a geographic spectacle: an almost sheer rising of land (to a height of approximately 344 feet, or over 100 metres, at the section of the ridge where the visitor centre is situated) created by the abrupt transition from, and differential movement between, one series of sedimentary rocks to another. The orientation of the escarpment, in relation to the prevailing north-easterly winds, creates a unique microclimate of winds and updrafts ensuring that this location is not only an attraction for geologists but also a key destination for gliders, hang-gliders, para-gliders and kite enthusiasts (the National Trust's boast, on its website, is that it is one of the best places in the country to fly a kite). The London Gliding Club is also situated at the base of the escarpment and so visitors to the Chiltern Hills Gateway visitor centre are regaled with the rather surreal sight of being able to observe planes and gliders taking off far below them (while also witnessing the occasional hang-glider or para-glider taking a running jump off the upper edge).

The majority of visitors are likely to arrive by car or coach, which then necessitates them approaching the building from the car park (which is subtly laid out, nestled into the existing contours of the site, and hence the cars remain hidden from view from most of the surrounding landscape). However, the approach to the building from the car park feels rather like walking up to the back door of the visitor centre since the front of the building feels as if it should surely be the one that faces, and embraces, the stunning views laid out so sumptuously below. This is not a building that you approach gradually, rather, it is suddenly there before you. The abruptness of the arrival and the sense that you are arriving at the rear of the building means that first impressions are not as convincing as they might otherwise have been. However, these first, less than positive, impressions are rapidly dispelled once the visitor has rounded the end of the building and the full relationship between building, sky and landscape is revealed.

Looking at the façade of the building it might be presumed that this building is little more than a simple, linear, glass box supporting an aerofoil-profiled, zinc-coated aluminium roof that appears to resemble an aeroplane or glider wing. The aerodynamic styling feels quite appropriate as the building gazes out over the antics of the Dunstable Gliding Club below. But in reality, these aeronautical touches are not merely aesthetic or whimsical gestures since they serve a functional purpose too, as its aerofoil form is what enables the roof to withstand the heavy wind loads that are inevitable on such an exposed site. The Chiltern Hills Gateway visitor centre is an attempt to create a small oasis of shelter and hospitality in this otherwise remote and windswept locale. (And what could be more civilised than settling down to a hot chocolate after an hour of vigorous kite-flying?).

Architecturally, the wind is also central to the building in another way as it employs a unique air-conditioning system that taps (literally) into the vigorous winds that would otherwise be merely buffeting the building. The architects designed something that, to the untrained eye, might appear nothing more than a modern looking, angular, Corten-steel sculpture poised on the edge of the escarpment. Instead it is, what has been termed by the architects, a 'wind-catcher'. The Corten steel, sculptural element is in fact the 'catching' part of a concealed air ventilation system: the wind catcher is then connected to the building via a subterranean, concrete tunnel or duct that is cut into the top of the escarpment and positioned at a depth of 2m below the surface of the ground. The air thus captured then flows a distance of approximately 90m into the visitor centre. In winter this air is warmed by its journey through the earth-enclosed tunnel since, at this level below ground, the air is typically a constant 12°C and hence is likely to be warmer than the outside air. In summer the reverse is true for at 12°C the air is likely to be cooler than the hot summer air, and so the building is naturally cooled. This natural air conditioning serves to reduce the running costs of the building since neither mechanical heating or cooling is required. The green credentials of the building are also evident in other ways, the FSC certification of the timber elements, the inclusion of a woodchip boiler and the use of rainwater harvesting to help flush the toilets. As such, it achieved the accolade of being a finalist in the Sustainable Building of the Year for 2007.

Once the visitor is finally inside the building, the wind is instantly forgotten the moment that the sliding doors of the main entrance close behind them. At this point the building is about one purpose and one purpose only: the luxurious enjoyment of a spectacular, panoramic landscape, viewed from a position of wind-free and warm comfort. The interior of the building (excluding the usual clutter of shop and cafe paraphernalia) is relatively self-effacing, permitting everything else to be subsumed to the visual lure of the landscape. It is a long, extrusion of a building, with spaces encountered sequentially (the admin., kitchen and toilets are scarcely perceived, from the inside, as being part of the same building). This is not a building where the inside and the outside merge, where one becomes the other and boundaries are erased, rather it is always perfectly clear that you are inside (and happy to be so) and are being generously protected from the elements. At the same time, it is expected that your attention will forever be on the far horizon: as the birds, kites and gliders soar around you, the building becomes the still centre of calm amidst these aerial acrobatics. To leave is to know that you will return, if only to attempt to improve your skill with a kite.

Chiltern Hills Gateway's entrance area and shop, looking towards the cafe

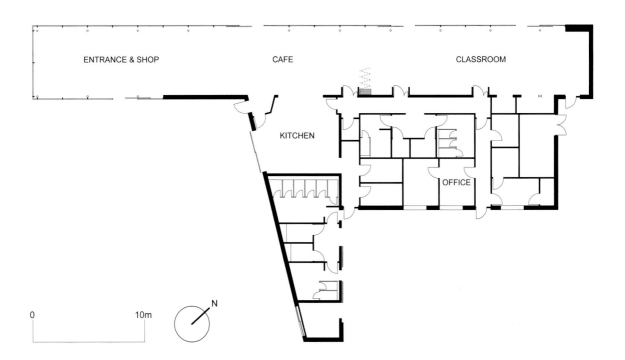

ENTRANCE & SHOP   CAFE   CLASSROOM

KITCHEN

OFFICE

0   10m

N

Plan of Chiltern Hills Gateway

Culloden Battlefield

KEY FACTS

FULL NAME

Culloden Battlefield

ARCHITECTS

Gareth Hoskins Architects

COMPLETION DATE

2008

COST

£9,400,000

COST/m²

£3,917

NEAREST POSTCODE

IV2 5EU

SELECTED AWARDS

Civic Trust Award – Communication 2009

GIA Award, Leisure/Retail Category – Winner 2008

RIAS Doolen Award, Best Building in Scotland – Special Mention 2008

IAA Design Award, Open Category – Shortlisted 2008

RIBA Award, Regional Award – Shortlisted 2008

Scottish Design Awards, Best Public Building – Finalist and Northern Exposure – Finalist 2008

The Wood Awards, Commercial and Public Access – Commended 2008

WAF Awards, Culture Category – Shortlisted 2008

Battle,
History
Nationalism

**Culloden Battlefield showing the corner
of the building closest to the battlefield site
with the moor beyond**

Like other battlefield sites (Bannockburn is another example) there are two issues at stake when designing a visitor centre: how to design a building that is respectful of a site where so many died and how to evoke a sense of place for the visitor, when very little or nothing remains to be seen. Relph talks of 'exceptional places' and in Chapter 1 the challenges of designing buildings for exceptional places are discussed. For battlefield sites it is the problem of designing buildings for *unexceptional* places but where *something exceptional* happened to have taken place. Culloden Moor is 8km/5 miles from Inverness in the highlands of Scotland; it is a windswept and desolate place, even today, although on a clear day you are rewarded with spectacular views of the distant mountains. The visitor centre and car park are located at the edge of the moor and so you must pass through, or alongside, the visitor centre to visit the battlefield site directly.

The building is very much a building of two halves: the facilities for the visitors located at the front of the building (reception, shop, cafe, toilets etc.), which is the part of the building clearly identifiable from the outside by its curved, shell roofs with clerestory lighting above it, and the rear part of the building containing the exhibition and orientation spaces of the building. This part has a flat roof from which visitors can view the battlefield site. There is, therefore, a strong sense of layering in this building, from front to back, and from more public (free to visit) to more private (for ticket holders and members only). In terms of architectural expression, the more public, facilities-focused parts are perhaps the more 'free-form' and expressive whereas the rear part is the more restrained and controlled.

Whether travelling by public or private transport, the visitor will arrive at the car park and walk the short distance to the visitor centre. The entrance is located at the corner of the building, the front more or less obscured from view by a stone wall. It is rather unusual to place entrances at corners of buildings, but in this case, it does provide the visitor with a choice: to enter the building or continue along the path along the building's flank in order to directly enter the battle site. Because of this choice, the would-be visitor is rewarded with a view of the moor, framed by the mass of the building to one side, the pedestrian bridge to the roof terrace above and to the other side. Even before the visitor has entered the building (or decided not to enter it) their ultimate destination is presented to them, and their choices clearly laid out. If they choose to walk directly to the moor, the path will lead them alongside the flank of the building: a stone façade with few windows. The wall forming this façade is made from Caithness stone and is inexplicably irregular, with some stones set back and others, apparently randomly, jutting forward. The overall impression is one of rhythm, texture and shadows; the protrusions of some stones provide a ledge on which small plants, such as ferns, have taken root adding to the texture. In fact, there is a rationale and logic to this apparently haphazard arrangement of stones: the pattern of projecting and recessed stones represents the numbers of Government and Jacobite casualties at Culloden. This wall is particularly interesting as it is just a small feature, a detail, that is likely to remain unnoticed by many of the visitors, but, in a very meaningful way it serves to fuse the building and the information about the battle into one seamless whole.

Assuming that the visitor decides not to bypass the centre and foregoes the experience of walking past the symbolically-laid stone wall, they will enter into the Culloden Battlefield visitor centre. Once inside, their immediate view will be of a long passage connecting the front to the back of the building,

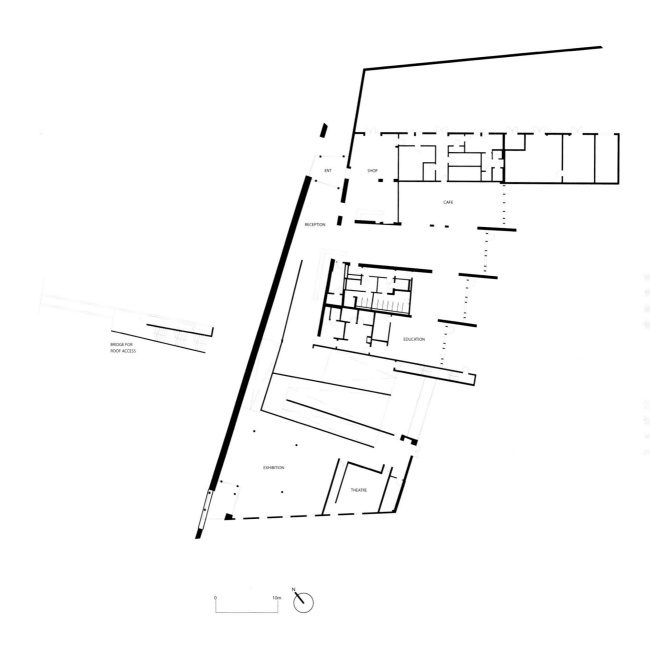

ENT

SHOP

CAFE

RECEPTION

EDUCATION

BRIDGE FOR
ROOF ACCESS

EXHIBITION

THEATRE

0   10m

N

Plan of Culloden Battlefield

top: Culloden Battlefield showing the
battlefield/moor framed in the distance from
the main entrance

above: One of Culloden Battlefield visitor
centre's long façades in horizontally-laid,
larch timber planks

which leads (mirroring the outside route) directly to the battlefield site. This path stretching ahead is rather dark and sombre, being faced with the same Caithness stone, and perpendicular to this route, in a bright and spacious contrast, are the reception, cafe and shop. Once again, the distinction between 'leisure' and 'remembrance' appears to be marked by the use of materials in the interior, as well as the exterior, surfaces. The material palette of the cafe and shops is wood and bright, clerestory-lit, expansive, white-painted walls. The routes into the exhibition area are stone clad (to the exhibition) or slate clad (to the battlefield). Is the use of materials intended to reflect the supposed mood of the visitor in some kind of architectural pathetic fallacy?

The cafe and multi-functional spaces, located beneath the curved shell roofs, are pleasant, spacious, light and lofty. The clerestory lights, wash light down the walls and accentuate the curves of the shell roofs (above the restaurant the underside of the shell roof is inscribed with the names of donors). Through the gable-ends of the shells, framed views towards the distant mountains are available, which can be gazed at while relaxing in the cafe.

The character of the exhibition part is quite different, as views outside are reduced or omitted entirely, and the whole area becomes more introspective. This is the section of the building that, as described at the beginning, has a flat, terrace roof. It also differs from the front section by being clad in horizontally-laid, larch timber planks, now weathered to a warm grey colour. In sunlight this can make the building seem almost luminous against the green of the moor and the hills and the sky beyond. Once through the exhibition, the battlefield site can be accessed via another exit/entrance, which leads directly onto the moor. Here, there is another archway, which supports a balcony and look-out

point from the roof terrace above. But this archway, like the one formed by the pedestrian bridge onto the roof terrace, serves the dual purpose of framing views to the site from the visitor centre.

The moor itself is, very simply, the moor, the battlefield – the National Trust for Scotland has attempted, as much as possible to return the battlefield site to the state it was in when the battle took place in 1746, even reversing the more modern drainage channels to ensure that the more marshy parts of the site, return to their original, sodden state. From this site, the visitor centre sits as a long, wooden-clad, silvery building, low and discrete in the landscape. Visitors tend to follow a set route around the site, which takes in the Memorial Cain as well as the clan stones for the dead of the highland clans. This is a simple building that does not attempt to be anything other than what it does, but it does this calmly, sensitively and with great attention to detail. And, in those places, where architecture and information/commemoration come together, it manages to rise above the ordinary, culminating in a very special building for a place that will forever be etched in many people's memories.

James Drummond, Duke of Perth

Culloden Battlefield, interior from the
approach to the main exhibition space

Fountains Abbey

KEY FACTS

FULL NAME

Fountains Abbey

ARCHITECTS

Cullinan Studio

COMPLETION DATE

1992

COST

£2,000,000

COST/m²

£1,250

NEAREST POSTCODE

HG4 3DZ

SELECTED AWARDS

Civic Trust Award 1996

BCI Awards Special Commendation 1993

RIBA Award 1993

Europa Nostra Medal of Honour 1992

top: Fountains Abbey view from the main entrance to the visitor centre showing the courtyard (and to the far left, the views to the Abbey tower in the distance)

above: Fountains Abbey showing the more private and 'rugged' external façade

This is a particularly significant visitor centre, in the context of this book, as it is the earliest one of those researched to have been built. Constructed in 1992, it is now 25 years old (the age at which some buildings have already reached the end of their 'life expectancy') and so it was particularly interesting to visit it and ask the following kinds of questions: From a typological perspective, does it share any formal, spatial and functional similarities with the later visitor centres in the book or is it more of an outlier? Was this the archetype that others were inspired by? Has it stood the test of time? Does it still feel contemporary?

The Fountains Abbey Visitor Centre, North Yorkshire, is located in a UNESCO World Heritage Site (designated as such since 1986). Fountains Abbey (founded in 1132 by Benedictine monks and closed in 1539 when Henry VIII ordered the Dissolution of the Monasteries) is one of the most picturesque ruins (along with Tintern Abbey in Monmouthshire, both of which were painted by J.M.W. Turner), as well as being the largest monastic ruins, in the county. However, the site later became incorporated into part of an expansive eighteenth-century landscape garden, Studley Royal Park, which is now considered to be one of the best surviving examples of a Georgian water garden in England.

Given the sensitivity and World Heritage status of the site (without question this would count as one of Relph's 'exceptional settings') Cullinan's visitor centre is located at some distance from the Abbey ruins. (It is about 400m, or 0.25 mile, 'as the crow flies' or about a 700m (0.5 mile) walk away), and therefore fits into the category of 'visitor centre at a distance from' its attraction (see Chapter 1). The visitor centre takes on the form of a medieval, monastic cloister, in other words an enclosed quadrangle surrounded on all sides by buildings and with an arcade or covered walkway around the inner edge of the buildings. Except that in the case of Fountains Abbey visitor centre, this cloister has had part of its surrounding buildings carved away: it is a partial or incomplete cloister. The reason for this is clear when standing in the middle of the quadrangle, since the portion that has been removed has been cut away at a tell-tale splayed angle. It has been removed in order to provide visitors with their first glimpse of the 'attraction' – not of the ruins themselves (they are set too low in the landscape to be seen from here) but of the very top of the Abbey tower. This tantalising view is framed by the buildings of the courtyard and is seen through, what would otherwise have been, a corner of the cloister (if this segment of the building had not been removed). We can therefore conclude that one of the common characteristics of many visitor centres in this book, using the buildings to frame specific views of the attraction, is already present in this early visitor centre. The framing of views to the top of the abbey tower is made all the more powerful by the fact that the entrance to the quadrangle is located on the diametrically opposite corner to the one that has been removed and so, upon entering the courtyard, the visitor is already oriented towards this view. The entrance-corner is articulated more subtly: the roof and the arcade continue to wrap around the cloister and so it is only a small section of the surrounding building that has been removed to permit entry. Consequently, prior to even entering the quadrangle, views to the attraction are beginning to be set up; the visitor is offered a series of staged views, each carefully building upon and developing the previous one. If two of the corners of the visitor centre's cloister are devoted to orienting the visitor and framing views to the abbey, then the other two corners take on more of a functional role, these being an education space and the cafe/restaurant.

There is a difference in the formal and material language of the outside of the buildings (outside the quadrangle) and the inside and this can be summed up simply as outside = 'hard' and inside the quadrangle/cloister = 'soft'. Formally, the outside of the buildings consists of steeply pitched roofs clad in slate coupled with thick, dry stone walls unbroken by any glazing (any windows on the outer side are high clerestory windows placed above the level of the dry-stone walls and permitting no views in). And so, the whole building appears to turn its back on the outside world (which was the original purpose of a cloister). Once the visitor has entered into the interior world of the quadrangle, the forms and materials change abruptly. Rather than being pitched roofs, the roofs become soft double-curves and are clad in lead rather than slate. The façades facing the interior of the courtyard are predominantly glazed, set behind the steel columns of the arcade and the seating surrounding the courtyard invites people to linger here and simply 'be' in this place.

Where these two geometries collide – the hard triangles of the outside and the double-curves of the interior courtyard – some interesting spatial volumes are produced, particularly at the corners of the quadrangle (where double-curves in one plane meet a double-curve, or triangle, in another plane). The cafe is one such spatially complex volume with soaring roof voids, sometimes featuring the curves and sometimes the steep pitches. Where the entire corner of the quadrangle buildings has been removed to frame the views towards the Abbey, this angled cutting away of space, through the double-curve of the interior roof, has produced a particularly dramatic, curved canopy, that seems as if it is almost pointing towards the visitors' destination.

Fountains Abbey showing the detail of the restaurant windows

These accentuations of the curves thus produced are perhaps also evocative of the repetitive arches of the vaulted cellarium of the Abbey buildings.

Materially, this building is one that blends opposites together. The steel frame is boldly modern and no attempt has been made to conceal it and yet it is then coupled with dry stone walls and, in places, cedar timber cladding (for solar shading). The overall effect is a modern, rural vernacular: a 'material motif' that appears again and again in many later visitor centres. Finally, the other impression that the visitor receives is a certain 'joie de vivre' among all this serious architecture. Wooden batons painted in primary colours articulate the undersides of the interior ceilings. These batons, in turn, support spotlights mounted on red-painted squares, superimposed on blue-painted circles. The effect is perhaps a little 'post-modern' (and probably the only aspect that now dates the building) and yet reminds the onlooker of an almost medieval, heraldic composition of round shields with crossed spears or swords. Overall this playful touch is one that serves to make the building feel very approachable and 'fun' to the visitor. It is perhaps no accident that on my visit the courtyard had been festooned with bunting, something that a more formidable architecture would repulse, but for this place it seemed at one with its general 'lived-in' and affectionate ambience.

Fountains Abbey showing the canopy roof marking the start of the path to the ruins

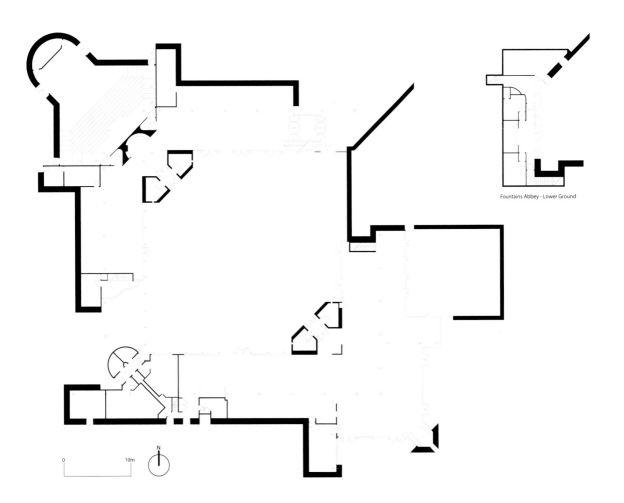

Fountains Abbey - Lower Ground

0   10m   N

Plans of Fountains Abbey

Giant's Causeway

KEY FACTS

FULL NAME

Giant's Causeway

ARCHITECTS

Heneghan Peng Architects

COMPLETION DATE

2012

COST

£9,425,000

COST/m²

£5,236

NEAREST POSTCODE

PA42 7AU

SELECTED AWARDS

Civic Trust Awards 2014

Royal Society of Ulster Architects Awards 2014

RIBA National Award 2013

RIBA Stirling Prize Shortlist 2013

Geology
Landscape
Water

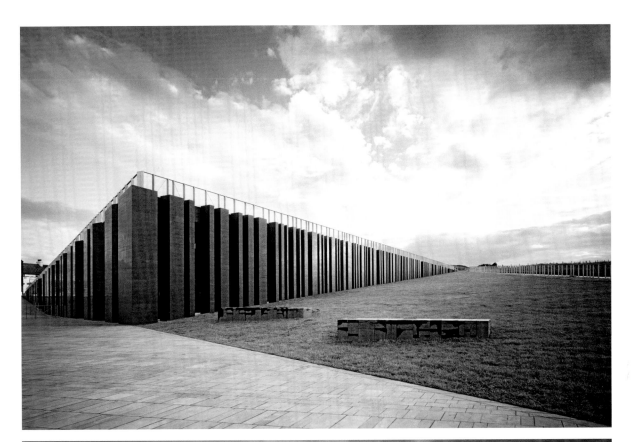

top: View of main façade of the Giant's Causeway visitor centre with the main entrance to the left
Source: Heneghan Peng Architects, photograph by Hufton & Crow

above: Long elevation of the Giant's Causeway visitor centre
Source: Heneghan Peng Architects, photograph by Hufton & Crow

This is a building without much of a sense of arrival, since it is simultaneously located on top of a slight hill, while also being built into the hillside; therefore it is almost invisible upon approach. The visitor is initially presented with a view of the building's corner, which is quite appropriate as this is a building that is all about angles and corners, obviously taking inspiration from the angular, hexagonal, basalt columns of the Giant's Causeway. From this approach, only two external walls of the building are visible (since the other two are interior, retaining walls), marching off into the distance on either side ('marching' since the walls are composed of thin, vertical columns of basalt stone, locally quarried in Kilrea, arranged in a slightly irregular pattern, that do appear to 'march' off into the distance). Standing in front of the corner-entrance, the building resembles a Renaissance drawing illustrating how to draw a two-point perspective, as each wall rapidly recedes towards its own vanishing point, punctuated by the quasi-regular spacing of the basalt columns. This point of convergence conceals the almost hidden entrance space, beyond which the actual building façade is set back, creating a sheltering external lobby space, before entering the building itself.

Once inside, the first thing that may capture the visitor's attention is the large expanse of ceiling. Ceilings are rarely planes in a building to be celebrated, and yet part of the subtle genius of this building lies in its folding, interior roof planes. The light is spectacular, since the sun penetrates the deep building-plan through long, generous roof lights. If the visitor is fortunate enough to visit after it has been raining, then the sunlight shining through the roof lights and raindrops creates delicate, lacy patterns of light on the adjacent concrete surfaces. The roof is based on the same non-rectangular grid that the rest of the building has been

planned around, and so the subtle angles are played out in the pre-cast concrete roof slabs, accentuated by the small, hanging lights at the centre of each roof grid – the only incongruity here is the fact that the suspended lights are cylinders, whereas everything else in the building echoes the angles of the hexagon. Why were the lights also not more angular? This resultant array of lights on the ceiling also serves to draw the visitors' attention to the subtle unevenness of the roof planes. The shifting planes of the ceiling reflect the changes in use of the open-plan space below and so the ceiling permits a shift from the soaring and majestic point at the rear of the building, marking the moment when the visitor embarks on their walk to the Giant's Causeway, to the much lower and intimate folds above the cafe space. It is in this way that an open plan space can shift mercurially to give a subtly different character to distinctive parts of it. (Despite the open plan nature of the building and the fact that it is typically full of people, the building is not at all noisy which might have been expected, given the abundance of very hard surfaces. It can only be concluded that this is due to the, either deliberate or accidental, acoustic properties of the shifting, folded planes of the roof.)

The angular grid has already been mentioned in the section above. This is perhaps one of the quirky oddities of the building; since it has not been planned on a typical, rectangular grid, but on a diamond-shaped grid produced by transforming the main axes of the building grid from right angles. The fact that buildings are rarely designed used non-rectangular grids should cause an expectation that, at the most, this might feel a little awkward and contrived or, at the least, that the placing of rectangular objects – such as tables – in an angular grid would be problematic. In fact, these

top: Giant's Causeway: detail of roof light

above: Main interior space of the Giant's Causeway visitor centre
Source: Heneghan Peng Architects, photograph by Hufton & Crow

shifted-grids are far subtler, and are noticeable more in the details and joints than at the larger scale. In the cafe, for example, even the tables have been custom designed to be at rakish angles, following the underlying grid in a building.

The building has been constructed with the same basalt stone from which the Causeway was formed and the visual quality of this stone (and hence the visitor centre) is a little surprising (the other 'quirkiness' of the building). In the sunlight, the stone appears to be a lighter brown, almost a dun colour and this 'version' of the building is the one that best reflects the primary colour of the Giant's Causeway stones. But when the façade of the building's exterior become wet, after rain for example, the stones can appear almost black in colour, and this 'version' of the building is the exact colour of the Causeway stones as the hexagonal basalt columns meet the crashing waves of the sea: it is the colour of this moment of the meeting between the Causeway and the sea, the colour not of stone but of the pairing of stone-plus-sea, it is the colour of liminality. Another surprising characteristic of the darker colour variation of the basalt stone of the visitor centre, is that when the stone is wet, it becomes almost luminously reflective, reflecting the landscape beyond it. If fortunate enough to visit on a day of rapidly changing weather, of bright sunshine alternating with rain, the visitor will experience two different buildings, in two different colour variations, each with their own characteristics (one more shiny, one more matt).

For a building that initially appears to be tucked away modestly in the side of the hill, it is a building that is about views, albeit views in tiny slivers. The angles of the façade's stones, and the narrow windows held between them, play a subtle trick upon the onlooker, whereby they can only see in/out of the one or two slivers of window directly in front of them and those windows that are further away disappear into the depth of the wall's thickness. And so, the effect, as the visitor walks parallel to the façade is one of a sequence of flickering views, as first one sliver of a view presents itself and another disappears, the overall effect is almost like a Muybridge animation of either the exterior landscape (if looking from the inside) or of visitors moving around (if viewed from the outside, looking in).

Given that this was an expensive building, it does not give the impression of being ostentatious (despite having what must be one of the most hard-wearing, stone façades ever specified). Rather, it comes across as being surprisingly modest and given its size, bulk and cost, it is a subtle and nuanced building. If any building, so far, has given the impression that the visitor centre is indeed a new type, rather than being a hybrid of other ones, it is this one. Each fragment seems effortlessly part of the whole: no part could be removed without the rest being left lacking. It is not a complex building, indeed it is quite simple, especially because of it being open plan, but its complexity is in its subtlety.

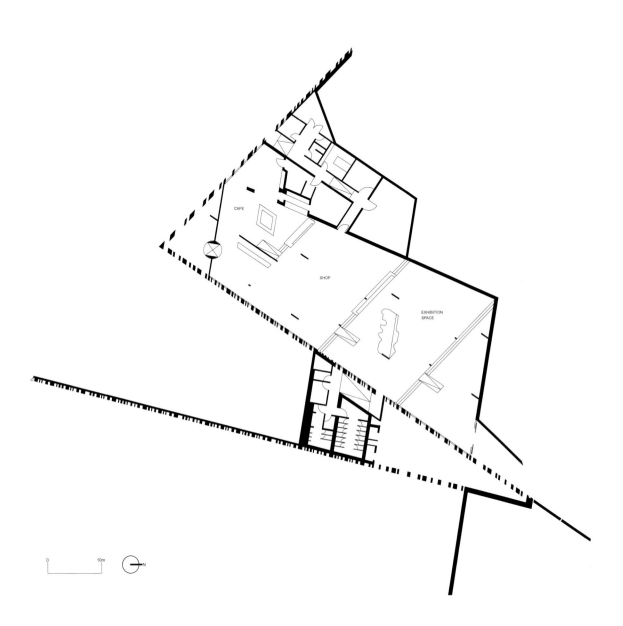

CAFE

SHOP

EXHIBITION
SPACE

0   10m   N

Plan of Giant's Causeway

The Giant's Causeway visitor centre at dusk
Source: Heneghan Peng Architects,
photograph by Hufton & Crow

Hafod Eryri

FULL NAME

Hafod Eryri

ARCHITECTS

Ray Hole Architects

COMPLETION DATE

2009

COST

£5,600,000

COST/m²

£8,960

NEAREST POSTCODE

LL55 4UL

SELECTED AWARDS

Unavailable

Geology
Landscape

top: Rear façade, Hafod Eryri, looking
towards the railway station

above: Hafod Eryri, showing walkers' entrance/
exit (as opposed to the train approach)

top: Hafod Eryri, showing the natural stone against the stone of the façade

above: Hafod Eryri: interior showing visitors silhouetted against the large picture windows

The name Hafod Eryri was selected for Snowdon's new visitor centre (opened to the public in June 2009) as a result of a public competition. 'Eryri' simply means Snowdonia whereas 'Hafod' is derived from the Welsh word for summer ('haf') and it indicates the higher pastures where sheep would be taken for the summer. As names go this is particularly apt since, due to the extreme weather in this location, the visitor centre and cafe is only open from the late spring to early autumn.

Similar to the Stonehenge visitor centre, there is a long history of previous 'accommodation' being erected on the top of Snowdon in order to provide some sort of shelter and sustenance to weary hikers having made their way to the summit. The most recent summit building was designed by the architect Clough Williams-Ellis in the 1930s (he is more commonly known for the Italianate village of Portmeirion) but this building had become extremely dilapidated due to the harsh environmental conditions on top of the mountain and it sorely needed demolition and replacement. The current building, designed by Ray Hole Architects, was the result of an architectural competition to replace the Clough Williams-Ellis building.

The architects had very little flexibility in terms of the options for siting the new building. Since there has been a train to the top of Snowdon Train since 1896, the new visitor centre could not be far from the train's terminus. Equally, because of the difficulty in transporting materials to the top of the mountain (only the train could be used; helicopters were considered dangerous and concrete, for example, could not be effectively pumped to the summit) the decision was taken to try to reuse and recycle as much of the old building as possible. An early decision was taken to build upon the existing foundations and to more or less keep to the same building envelope/

volume as the previous building. (Eventually, when the old building was demolished and its condition found to be far poorer than predicted, very little of the building material was in a good enough condition to be reused).

The form of the building has been likened to a weaver's shuttle or torpedo because of its low profile and curved walls and roof. In reality, this is a true case of 'form follows function' since the shape of the building needed to be able to withstand winds of up to 150mph, as well as exceptionally heavy snow loads, when the temperature on the summit can reach −20°C. Specialist software was therefore used to model the building's overall shape as well as to ensure that, as the building's steel frame was erected section by section, each incomplete stage in the process was also able to withstand extreme winds. The resultant form of the building is a low, single-storey building that is relatively long and thin and with pronounced, curved corners. In winter it is designed to 'go into hibernation', having galvanised steel shutters that come down to entirely cover the windows. The external balustrading was designed to be dismantled and stored: the whole building literally 'hunkers down' and waits out the season.

The external walls of the building have been faced in extremely durable, local granite sourced from the Cwt y Bugail quarry in Blaenau Ffestiniog. In order to reduce the construction time on site (the extreme weather also meant that the window of time during which onsite work could take place was only between April and October) each of the granite blocks was prepared and shaped prior to being taken up the mountain. The stone courses consist of blocks of stone that are cut to the same height but with irregular lengths and their faces left rough to make it feel more rustic (or 'rock-like'), but then each subsequent stone-course varies in height giving an impression of sedimentary rock deposits (this 'strata-effect' is further echoed inside with the horizontal layering of the Welsh Oak cladding).

In terms of the experience of the building, this is probably a building that engenders the widest possible range of emotions among its visitors, depending upon how they arrive at the building and on the weather conditions at the top of the mountain. For those who arrive via the historic, narrow gauge steam railway, having sat in warmth and relative comfort for the journey, the arrival at the visitor centre on top of the building is still an exhilarating one, but merely forms part of the on-going journey. For those who arrive on foot, the experience of arriving at the visitor centre is quite different. Many of them are in need of a comfort break and a rest, not to mention a hot drink (if the weather is cold). For them, the building is the end point to an often-challenging physical test of ability and represents a chance to recover before attempting the walk back down. And here is where the weather also makes a difference to people's experience of arriving on the top of the mountain: on an inclement day, if people have walked through the cold or wet to get to the summit, then this will be quite a different building experience than if it is a bright sunny day. If it is particularly windy then the need to get out of the wind will also be uppermost in hikers' minds. In bad weather the building's role as refuge and place of relief subsumes any architectural significance.

Like the Giant's Causeway building (and perhaps to a greater degree), this is a building that changes entirely depending on the weather. The photographs show the building at its most atmospheric. When I was there, it was misty and foggy; there were no views to speak of and, as a consequence, I experienced a quite intimate relationship between the building, the cloud and me. The swirling fog limited any views whilst simultaneously focusing my whole attention on the building, which felt cold, wet and looked darker than I had seen it appear in other photographs. The granite felt as if it truly was part of the mountain, as if it had somehow been raised up and assembled into this rough, lump of a building (the fog meant that I could never really get a good overview of it). On the surface of the stones moss was beginning to grow: the building and the landscape beginning to fuse. Then moving inside, from the cold, damp exterior, the main impression was one of warmth, wood and golden light, of being embraced and protected. On a clear day, with the spectacular views from the window it must feel as if you are on top of the world.

The Welsh National Poet, Gwyn Thomas, was commissioned to write a poem to mark the opening of the new summit building and it is inscribed on the surfaces of the building and its windows. Not many buildings have poems written in honour of their opening; it reinforces how significant place and landscape are to this building. This could have been a controversial building had the architect got this balance wrong, but it literally does feel as if the mountain and the building are one.

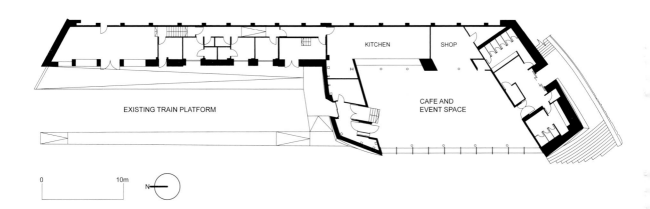

EXISTING TRAIN PLATFORM

KITCHEN

SHOP

CAFE AND
EVENT SPACE

0   10m

N

Plan of Hafod Eryri

Jodrell Bank

FULL NAME

Jodrell Bank

ARCHITECTS

Feilden Clegg Bradley Studios

COMPLETION DATE

2012

COST

£4,700,000

COST/m²

£4,747

NEAREST POSTCODE

SK11 9DL

SELECTED AWARDS

Unavailable

Science

Jodrell Bank, façade of Planet Pavilion showing part of the contour map of the invisible radio sky

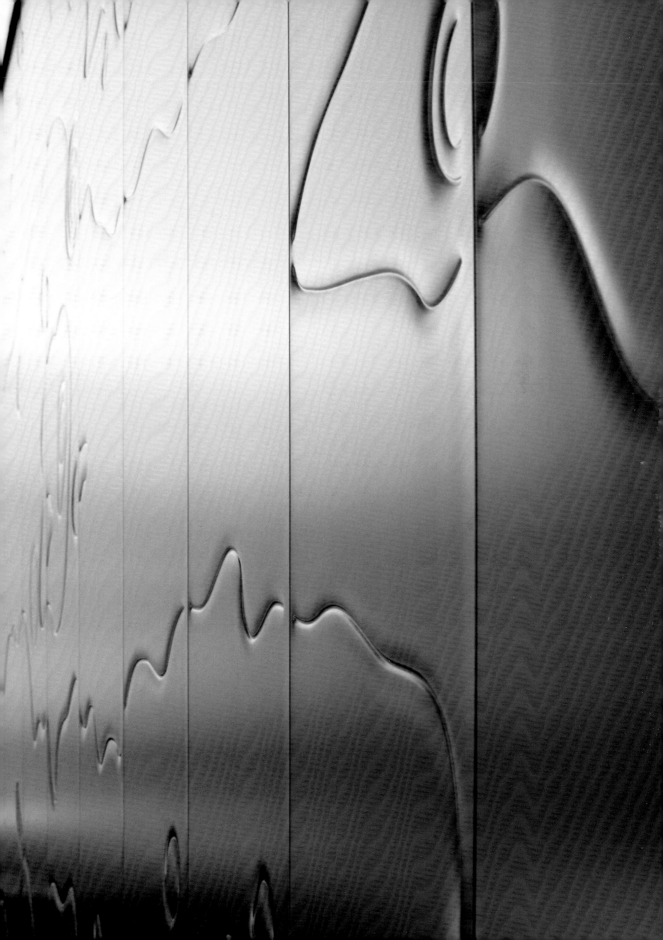

Jodrell Bank is an interesting visitor centre, as it rather turns the idea on its head that visitor centres are first and foremost about place and landscape. It is certainly true that the Jodrell Bank visitor centre could not be located anywhere else in the world, as it exists precisely because the Jodrell Bank Observatory (originally the Jodrell Bank Experimental Station) is there. But the siting of the Jodrell Bank Observatory, located in the small village of Lower Withington, Cheshire, came about more through happenstance than by grand design. At the beginning of the Second World War the University of Manchester purchased three fields in the village for use by its Botany Department and at the end of the war, Bernard Lovell, then a physicist at the University, was granted permission to place some army surplus radar equipment on the site for a mere two weeks in order to carry out some experiments and the rest, as they say, is history.

The visitor centre is reached via the A535 and en route the visitor is rewarded with a spectacular view of the Lovell Telescope (The 'Mark I' telescope), whose dish boasts an impressive 76.2 metres diameter and hence towers above the relatively flat, and arguably unremarkable, rural landscape. But upon finally reaching the visitor centre the visitor is, to misappropriate the words of Philip Johnson, somewhat 'unceremoniously dumped in front of it.' Any anticipation wrought by the appearance of the Lovell Telescope is hardly realised in the ritual of arrival, which is brusque, and to the point. The visitor centre, designed by Feilden Clegg Bradley Studios, consists of three separate pavilions placed thoughtfully around the site: the Planet Pavilion (housing the reception, cafe, gift shop and small exhibition area); the Space Pavilion (larger exhibition, 'classroom pod' and events space); and the latest addition, the Star Pavilion (flexible multi-purpose space/auditorium). It is the largest of the three, the Planet Pavilion, which is first encountered by the visitor.

All of the buildings are variations on a theme: low, long, sleek, black and almost featureless. Together they consist of three relentlessly modern, almost industrial, black boxes of varying proportion and set into the landscape. 'Almost featureless' is not quite accurate though, as the entrance façade of the Planet Pavilion, which faces the car park and hence greets new arrivals, is far from 'featureless'. On this one façade, the plain metal panels are instead inscribed with a set of swirling, dancing contour lines, covering the entire length and height of

Cafe and exterior terrace area at the end of the Planet Pavilion

the façade, representing a map of the invisible radio sky. This strip of sky shows some of the brightest objects in the radio sky and an information board placed in front of the building helps the visitor to pick out these objects, one by one, on the surface of the building. At a time in which ornament on buildings is rare, such an embellishment comes as an agreeable surprise.

The first-time visitor enters the Planet Pavilion and is rapidly processed via the reception, then led through a dark (the colour black being an ongoing theme), narrow passageway lit by an array of fibre-optic 'hairs' dangling from the ceiling, through to the Orrery Exhibition Room and then out into the rest of the site. Part of the brief for this visitor centre was about rationalising the rest of the site and the network of circulation paths around it. As a consequence of this master planning exercise, behind the relatively simple, black boxes, there are some rather clever games being played.

The alignments of the buildings are all orientated to the Lovell Telescope, which is the metaphorical lodestone of the site. Visually dominant, it dwarfs everything around it, and so everything else is placed logically in relation to this single, governing object. The long axis of the Planet Pavilion terminates at the centre of the telescope, so that the cafe and associated terrace at the end of the pavilion perfectly align to the telescope, literally framing its views. At the end of this alignment (which begins to feel unscientifically akin to ley lines) is located the spiral maze of the 'galaxy garden'. In contrast, the smaller Space Pavilion, located far closer to the telescope, is positioned with its long façade facing the telescope, its entrance and two flanked walls subtly aligned to invisible radial lines connecting the building to the focal point of the dish. It is not surprising that the buildings all orient themselves towards, and pay homage to the telescope, since that is really the point of the site.

However, there is one additional corollary of such careful building orientation. As mentioned already, the buildings themselves are clad in black metal panels, blank and featureless (apart from the radio sky map on the front of the Planet Pavilion). These black façades act as mirrors in which reflections of the telescope can be revealed. Where the black metal

of the façades gives way to glazing, in the right light, reflections of the telescope suddenly spring into life. These buildings are essentially all about reflections, which can be held as being particularly apt since one of the first experiments carried out in the early days of Jodrell Bank was the detection of echoes from meteors by the reflection of radio waves.

If these reflections explain the 'blackness' of the façades, what explains their boxiness? Is it simply the most rational, 'scientific' form for a scientific site and client? Perhaps. But again, there are conceivably more subtle compositional games being played and the clue is to be found in the buildings' plans. It is an accepted architectural compositional technique to set the single circle or curved element against the square or rectilinear plan, so that each may be emphasised in contrast to the other. In the Planet Pavilion the circle is to be found in the Orrery Exhibition Room, in which model planets circle the sun as part of a five-metre diameter, mechanical orrery. Later, in the Space Pavilion, the circle in plan becomes more evident in the guise of the bright yellow circular 'classroom pod' placed in the centre of the exhibition area. Once psychologically primed to see these circles in plan, the reason for the black boxiness of the pavilions becomes suddenly apparent: it is the perfect foil for the white curves of the telescopes. Compositionally, white is set against black and the curve or sphere is set against the line, rectangle or box: each element is presented in contrast to the other, serving to highlight and promote each other through their formal differences.

Of course, there might be one final reason for the unrelenting blackness of the pre-fabricated façade cladding panels. In Stanley Kubrick's film *2001: A Space Odyssey*, mysterious black monoliths appear periodically. The meaning of these featureless, black shapes has been debated but they are thought to perhaps represent the potentially transformative power of making contact with an alien race. Given that the Lovell Telescope is also engaged in SETI (the Search for Extraterrestrial Intelligence) observations, is it perhaps too fanciful to imagine that the façade cladding panels might represent ranks of '2001' monoliths standing in silent salute to the telescope: black, silent and enigmatic, waiting for alien first contact?

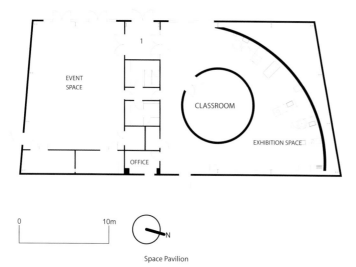

EVENT
SPACE

1

CLASSROOM

EXHIBITION SPACE

OFFICE

0   10m

N

Space Pavilion

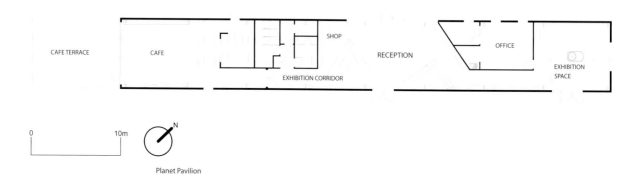

CAFE TERRACE   CAFE   SHOP   RECEPTION   OFFICE   EXHIBITION SPACE

EXHIBITION CORRIDOR

0   10m

N

Planet Pavilion

Plans of Jodrell Bank

top: Photograph of the reflections of the
Lovell Telescope in the windows of the
Space Pavilion

above: Reflections of the Lovell Telescope in a
building's façade

Richard III

FULL NAME

King Richard III Visitor Centre

ARCHITECTS

Maber

COMPLETION DATE

2014

COST

£4,000,000

COST/m²

£3,249

NEAREST POSTCODE

LE1 5DB

SELECTED AWARDS

Construction News National Awards Project of the Year (under £10m category) – Winner 2015

RICS National Project of the Year – Finalist 2015

RIBA East Midlands Regional Award – Winner 2015

FBE East Midlands Project of the Year 2014

Pro-Con Awards, Large Non-residential – Winner 2014

Archaeology
History
Royalty
Battle

**Richard III visitor centre showing the space
around Richard's burial site**

top: Richard III visitor centre showing reflections of the old school buildings in the new

above: Richard III visitor centre, looking
towards the main entrance/shop

Until recently, Richard III was the only English monarch whose final resting place was unknown. Now his story is well known as the archaeological find of the century: *The King in the Car Park*. The story of his discovery originates in 2012 when the University of Leicester Archaeological Service (ULAS) undertook a series of excavations in and around the site of the current visitor centre. In a car park, belonging to Leicester County Council, skeletal remains were subsequently found: a site that would have formed part of the choir section of the Greyfriars Church, which previously stood there. At this point, Leicester County Council took the (prescient) decision to buy an adjacent building, a former grammar school (the Alderman Newton School) that had become vacant, with a view to it possibly becoming a visitor centre. At this stage, however, the skeletal remains had yet to be identified as even belonging to Richard III and so the purchase of the school buildings, represented some risk to the council.

Once the remains had been identified (using DNA from Richard's known descendants), there was only a small window of opportunity to have the new visitor centre built in time for the planned reinterment of Richard's remains, which was eventually performed in Leicester Cathedral in 2015, less than 100m from where he was discovered. Given the short timescales involved in the project, the usual methods of procurement (most likely this would have been an architectural competition) were omitted, and instead Maber Architects were selected on the basis of having a proven track record with Leicester City Council and were appointed using a design and build contract. The visitor centre was completed in time for the reinterment and has since been passed to the King Richard III Visitor Centre Trust who run and manage the facility.

The complexity of this project should not be underestimated (timescale, procurement and budget aside). First, there was the challenge of reusing the existing school's listed buildings; next, of responding to the wider context (the site is located within the Cathedral Guildhall Conservation Area); of making reference, and drawing attention, to the previous Greyfriars Church on the site, whose orientation was key to finding Richard's resting place; of

creating a visitor centre whose primary 'attraction' is essentially nothing more than a hole in the ground (the car park burial site) and, finally, to somehow achieve all of this with the correct degree of sensitivity and dignity as befits a past monarch. Given the many things that could have gone wrong with this project, it is remarkably successful in its execution.

The entrance to the visitor centre is located off a pedestrianised lane, in front of Leicester Cathedral and forming one edge of the Cathedral Gardens. It forms a relatively subtle, urban intervention, sited on part of the former Grammar School yard (and part of the Greyfriars churchyard before that), and simply consists of a deep canopy bridging the gap between the two adjacent, listed buildings; the glazed façade of the reception/retail area is set further back beneath this canopy. Walking up to it does not convey much of a sense of arrival (difficult to achieve in such a constrained, inner-city site), and its subtle treatment of the front elevation might suggest any number of functional uses. Once through the doors, however, and it is clear that this is a visitor centre.

As soon as the visitor has become oriented in the welcome area, their attention is drawn to the fact that the reception/retail area appears to be intersected by a different space, separated by glass and raised up at a slightly higher level. This, almost, 'building-within-a-building', is part of the new-build portion of the visitor centre and been erected over the approximate choir section of the Greyfriars Church. Spatially, it is intended to represent the boundaries of the past church, since no above-ground traces are evident, and functionally it serves as an approach to the burial location of Richard. This, however, is a space that is seen but not directly entered, since the visitor route leads by ramp to a set of galleries about the life, politics and reign of Richard III (the second-floor exhibitions describe the science and detective story behind the discovery). The visitor eventually finds their way back to this space, that is at the heart of everything, and yet, sequentially is the visitor's final destination. The appearance of the 'resurrected' Greyfriars Church space was carefully considered to reflect materials that would have been familiar to the original church:

local limestone, sourced from a quarry less than 25 miles away, and locally sourced English Green Oak.

For a building constructed so rapidly, it is surprising to find such attention to detail, as evident in the choice of local materials. But these touches are found throughout the building. For example, when standing in the new structural, frameless glazed viewing gallery, looking down over the copper roof of the new exhibition space superimposed on the site of the Greyfriars Church, two small, metal finials in the shape of roses (the white rose was an emblem of the House of York) can be espied. More evidence of painstaking design is in the views into and around the centre, where care was taken (and with the advice of the archaeologists) to try to include views that would have been present in the past. As the architect observed, 'Visitor centres are often a great vehicle for architects to apply their skills with real meaning, which can be lacking in day-to-day practice.' And it is evident that the meaningfulness of this commission was very present in their minds throughout the design.

Finally, the visitor's journey through the building concludes at the site of Richard's burial, the (in)famous car park space. Again, how do you give such a space dignity? And how do you display what is, in effect, just a hole in the ground, without slipping into absurdity? In fact, this is probably the highlight of the building. The inspiration behind this room was for the roof to appear, not only floating, but also as if it were in the process of being lifted, metaphorically lifting the lid from the top of a tomb. The space is small and relatively intimate, and a sloping, copper ceiling dips down towards the gravesite, as if pointing to the spot where Richard was found. Where the copper ceiling slopes upwards towards the edges of the stone wall, the ceiling and wall appear not to meet, separated, as they are, by an almost invisible glass band (detailed so that no joints are visible). The lighting effect that this relationship of horizontal slit, and reflective, sloping ceiling produces on a sunny day is quite extraordinary, the light simply bounces around the space. The only indication of where Richard would have lain, in the hole below (sealed beneath a glass floor) is shown by a faint, visual projection of his bones in the exact position in which they were found. Seeing this space in photographs, prior to visiting, it would be easy to assume that it might be gaudy and ostentatious: in reality, it is far more subtle and delicate.

Leicester Cathedral framed by the entrance to the Richard III visitor centre

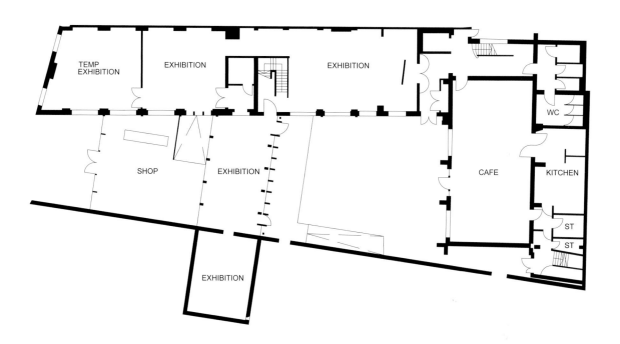

TEMP
EXHIBITION

EXHIBITION

EXHIBITION

WC

SHOP

EXHIBITION

CAFE

KITCHEN

ST

ST

EXHIBITION

0   10m

N

Plan of Richard III

Rosslyn Chapel

FULL NAME
Rosslyn Chapel

ARCHITECTS
Page\Park Architects

COMPLETION DATE
2011

COST
£3,800,000

COST/m²
£8,482

NEAREST POSTCODE
EH25 9PU

SELECTED AWARDS
Scottish Design Awards – Commendation 2013

Religious
Culture

top: Rosslyn Chapel visitor centre showing the criss-crossing, double roof beams

above: Rosslyn Chapel visitor centre looking out towards the approach walk and the doorway in the original wall (inspiration for the roof beams)

It is rather a shame to state this, but it is undoubtedly true, that few people had heard of the Rosslyn Chapel, in Scotland, prior to the release of the book and subsequent film, by Dan Brown, *The Da Vinci Code*. As well as being the setting for the climax of the book, the chapel was also used as a film location in 2005 and, as a consequence, many more people have now visited the chapel than would otherwise have done so (and hence the need to cater for the unforeseen increase in numbers). The reality is, however, that despite the recent surge in interest in the chapel, it had been a visitor attraction for hundreds of years, and not for the reasons given in Dan Brown's book, but because it is, quite simply, a remarkable architectural curiosity. Construction of the chapel began in 1456 and it was intended as a private place of worship for the Sinclair family, in whose ownership it remains to this day. But the chapel defies any conventional, architectural classification: it is noteworthy for the profusion of stone carvings that adorn every possible surface, every structural element, every window or doorframe. There is no place untouched by the stonemason's hand, and the effect is rather overwhelming. For some, it is clearly a place of wonder, delight and discovery (and, indeed, it is quite a pleasurable activity to search for some of the more obscure and unusual carvings) but for others the chapel borders on being a chaotic and eccentric folly. There is no doubt, however, that in the architectural and ecclesiastic history of the UK, Rosslyn Chapel occupies a very special niche.

The visitor centre is sited alongside the chapel, partly reusing an existing eighteenth-century stable building, through which the visitors pass to access the chapel. The existing stable building is a simple, stone-built, vernacular building with a tiled, pitched roof and plain, stone gables. This building is as simple and unremarkable as the chapel is singular and quirky. The form of the new building, by Page\Park architects, appears initially to take more of its inspiration from this plain and simple vernacular stable-block than from the chapel: its form also has a pitched roof, is orientated the same way as the stable building and is approximately the same height as, and overall massing of, the original building. And yet this is where the similarities end, for the new visitor centre building is as far from being a copy of a vernacular rural building as can be imagined, it is more as if it is a pure, abstract form, derived from the original, and yet transcending it. And transcendence is quite appropriate here, since the roof of the new visitor centre seems to float above its walls, as it protrudes beyond the building's façade at either gable end and the impression of floating is further reinforced by high-level clerestory windows positioned between the walls and the roof.

The approach to this building is one of the most satisfying of all the visitor centres in this book. As you arrive in the car park, you see nothing of the visitor centre despite it being only a short walk away, then approaching on foot, you turn into the lane and suddenly there it is, right in front of you. The situation of the building is slightly higher than the car park, and it is approached via a gentle incline, the visitor's attention firmly fixed on this elevated view ahead. The space in front of the visitor centre is clearly defined by walls on either side (one old, one new), and so the space in front takes on the feeling of a small plaza, bestowing a certain grandeur on the walk to the entrance that it would otherwise not have. On approaching, the similarities and differences between the old stable building and the new visitor centre are clearly read: the formal relationship and the material juxtapositions are immediately revealed to the approaching visitor.

top: Rosslyn Chapel visitor centre, overhanging roof that appears to 'float'

above: Photograph looking upwards/towards, via a gentle incline, the main entrance of the Rosslyn Chapel visitor centre

First Floor

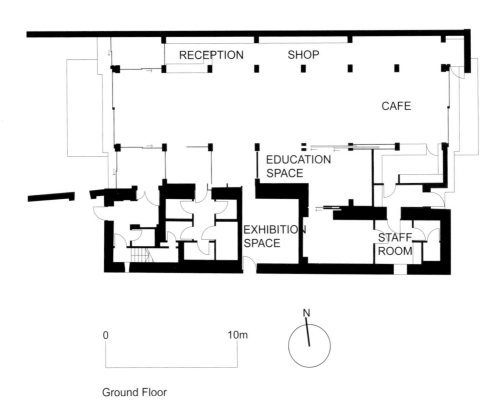

0   10m

Ground Floor

Plans of Rosslyn Chapel

Perhaps the only surprise is that the entrance is not located at the centre of the front façade, beneath the apex of the roof, as might be expected, but rather shifted to one side, subtly breaking the symmetry of the building.

Moving inside the building, the impression is immediately one of lightness and elegance almost as if the roof is floating, hovering above the walls. This is not a complex building; it is effectively a single – and relatively small – volume that is subdivided into different functional areas (the welcome desk, the exhibition area, the shop and the cafe). And yet, the next observation (after the lightness of the roof and elegance) is that it is a small space upon which has been lavished considerable thought and attention to detail.

The impression of the elegance of the roof arises from the unusual structural beams/rafters. Rather than single, solid, heavy, timbers, the roof is an unusually complex arrangement of small-section, double-beams that criss-cross, weaving in and out of each other, along the length of the roof. It is the design of the roof, above all else that gives hints and suggestions of ecclesiasticism since they are rather reminiscent of the diagonal ribs of groined vaulting. In fact, the architects' inspiration for the roof beams came from a carved pediment above a doorway in the original wall. This carving represents a series of nested triangles, decreasing (or increasing) in size and between each successive triangle, the space is filled with tiny crosses. According to the architects, the concept of the roof beams was that it should seem as though this two-dimensional carving had been extruded along the extent of the roof.

This lightness of touch is not to be found throughout the building as below the height of the clerestory windows, are a series of chunky, over-sized, rustic, green oak columns (and side aisles beyond). The texture of this wood is intended to be noticed and marvelled at (touched even) for they are rough, uneven and have fissures running along their lengths (although their sheer size dispels any anxiety that these cracks might affect their structural performance). These columns and beams of tactile, textured timber sit upon a floor that is surfaced in relatively rough, dark stone, surprising in a space that is generally light and bright. And so the contrast with the lightness of the roof, can only be intentional: that the heaviness of these timbers, emphasise the lightness of the roof by means of the visual contrast between the two. This is further reinforced by the darkness of the stone with the white-painted plaster of the roof. The effect is uplifting, as the eyes of the visitors are drawn towards the ceiling (and potentially to the heavens beyond); it is this subtle emphasis on the roof, sky and above that lends an ecclesiastical quality to the space. This building takes its simplicity and honesty from the vernacular building, and the uplifting emphasis on the roof, the allusion to groin vaulting, the side aisles and the attention to detail, from the chapel itself. It is a small, but very beautifully designed and constructed building.

Stonehenge

KEY FACTS

FULL NAME

Stonehenge Visitor Centre

ARCHITECTS

Denton Corker Marshall

COMPLETION DATE

2013

COST

£9,500,000

COST/m²

£6,271

NEAREST POSTCODE

SP4 8NU

SELECTED AWARDS

Europa Nostra Award 2016

Michael Middleton Civic Trust Special Award 2016

AIA Jørn Utzon Award for International Architecture 2014

RIBA South West Award 2014

Archaeology

top: Stonehenge, showing one of the short façades, looking towards the exhibition side of the building (the wooden 'box')

above: Stonehenge, showing the 'erosion' motif detailing around the windows

top: Stonehenge visitor centre, showing the view between the two 'boxes' (glass/retail to the right and wooden/exhibition to the left) and looking towards the small ticket booth nestling between

above: Stonehenge, showing spindly, irregular columns in silhouette

What is striking about the Stonehenge visitor centre is that it is sited about one and a half miles from Stonehenge (compared to 800m or 0.5 mile for Fountains Abbey and 1km, or 0.7 mile for the Giant's Causeway) and like Fountains Abbey and the Giant's Causeway there is no visible relationship between the visitor centre building and the site. In each case, the building is invisible from the attraction and vice versa. The visitor centre is sited off a private road that used to be the A344 (a public road that used to run mere metres from the heel stone of the ancient monument) but in 2013, during the construction of the visitor centre, this section of the A344 was dug up and grassed over. Another section of the road was retained to be used as an access way, connecting the visitor centre to the ancient monument by a visitor shuttle-bus service. The permanent closure of this section of the A344 has undoubtedly improved the siting and presentation of the stones. Any sense of arrival, therefore, is very low-key, arriving almost certainly by car or coach from a roundabout on the A303 and a short stretch to the visitor centre located off another roundabout known as Airman's Corner. The visitor arriving by car will pass in front of the visitor centre in order to park and then approach the visitor centre from its right flank. The better approach, from the perspective of the building, is actually from the coach park, approaching the visitor centre from its left flank, as each give a different perspective of the building. The building as viewed from the car park is more foreshortened, squat and with the curve of the roof, less emphatic. In contrast the building as viewed from the coach park is more dramatic, with the gentle sweep of the roof mirroring the undulating landscape or perhaps invoking a bird in flight.

The diagram of the building is a very simple one: a lightweight, gently curved roof supported by a forest of irregular, skinny columns forming a floating canopy over a pair of disconnected boxes (primarily retail and museum) with a small ticket booth nestling between the two. The execution of the building however, is far from simple as a plethora of details have been included in the realisation of the building that constantly vie for attention so that the simplicity of the diagram fades slightly. The first,

most striking detail, is the contrast between the very lightweight and elevated roof (perhaps canopy is a better term, as it is not functioning as a roof in the strictest sense of the word) and the forest of spindly, irregular, thin steel columns. The effect is almost one of an optical illusion, rather like the way that a 'magician's assistant' may be suspended on two chairs and then, as each chair is removed, the assistant remains, apparently 'floating'. There is a sense, with this building, that the entanglement of columns, oriented every which way, feel as if they are poised, waiting to tumble down, (like a child's game of spillikins, to use another analogy) in which case, the 'audience' would be waiting with baited breath to see if the canopy would succeed in levitating or not.

Beneath this almost floating, almost magical, tent-like roof are a pair of reassuringly solid boxes. One is clad in vertical timber boards, the other glazed and highly reflective. These are a pair, identical in size and scale, but with a contrasting materiality. The mirrored half is pristine and 'finished', its aesthetic is one of transparency and reflections of the landscape; in contrast, its sibling wooden building appears rather 'jagged', either half-finished or somehow 'eroded', and 'incomplete' in just the same way that the glazed block is presented as perfectly formed and finished. The glass block houses the gift shop, cafe and educational space whereas the wooden block contains the interpretation area, toilets and membership office. Between the two is a tiny cube of a ticket booth. The bifurcation of the two blocks acts almost as a funnel, channelling the visitor towards the ticket booth. Although the facing planes of the glass and wooden blocks are parallel, the perspective view from either side of the building makes these faces appear angled from each other, as though literally funnelling the visitor's path and gaze. But the visual illusion works both ways, from the entrance it appears to funnel/direct the visitor's gaze towards the monument (even though it is out of sight, set over a slight rise in the landscape), if the visitor stands on the other side, looking back towards the approach path, away from the stones, the effect is reversed and their view appears to be focused in the opposite direction.

The formal elements: the lightweight, floating roof, the forest of irregularly angled skinny columns and the two, materially distinct, yet formally matched boxes huddling beneath have been discussed. Equally the material palette, the glass box and its rustic timber counterpart, and the steel of the curiously proportioned columns have been described. What remains unmentioned is the building's ornamentation. There is a surprising number of 'decorative' elements for what is a modern building. Standing beneath the canopy, looking towards the sky, the edges of the floating roof are perforated with a pattern of 'pixelated erosion'. This pattern appears only on the very outer edge of the canopy and, on the one hand, serves to make the edge, which is remarkably thin anyway, feel all the more insubstantial, as if the abrupt distinction between canopy and sky is rendered less defined and more continuous. Again, there is a sense of 'erosion' being suggested, as if the material of the building is starting to weather away, revealing fragments of the sky through the metal. This decorative 'erosion' motif is further echoed in the treatment of the openings of the rustic, timber museum block. Where there are openings or windows in the museum block (and this includes the entrances to the toilets), the timbers are cut at different lengths around the opening, creating a jagged, irregular edge to the 'gap'. Sometimes these are literally openings, entrances and exits but sometimes they are the edges to windows, framing a large expanse of seamless glazing behind the raw edge. The effect is rather disconcerting, as some of the windows can seem rather like a gaping maw, surrounded by uneven teeth …

Are these 'motifs of erosion' meant to represent the erosion of the stones at Stonehenge? Are the skittish angles of the columns meant to echo the occasional rakish angles of some of the upright stones of the henge, as they have gradually tilted and settled over the centuries? Does the forest of columns represent the now missing wooden posts, theorised by some to have been placed in the 56 'Aubrey holes' around the stone henge, and believed to date from one of the earliest phases of Stonehenge? (There are approximately 56, give or take a few, columns placed around each of the square blocks). I confess, that despite some striking moments, the overall effect was one of mystery – why were certain design steps taken? It is almost as mysterious as Stonehenge itself.

Architects' development sketches for Stonehenge
Source: Denton Corker Marshall Architects, used with permission

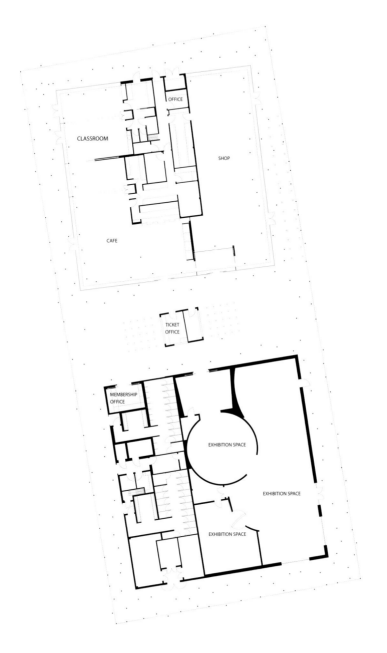

CLASSROOM

OFFICE

SHOP

CAFE

TICKET
OFFICE

MEMBERSHIP
OFFICE

EXHIBITION SPACE

EXHIBITION SPACE

EXHIBITION SPACE

N

0   10m

Plans of Stonehenge

The Sill

KEY FACTS

FULL NAME

The Sill Landscape Discovery Centre

ARCHITECTS

Jane Darbyshire and David Kendall

COMPLETION DATE

2017

COST

Not yet available

COST/m²

Not yet available

NEAREST POSTCODE

NE47 7AW

SELECTED AWARDS

Unavailable

Archaeology
Geology
Landscape

Architects' visualisation of The Sill
Source: JDDK Architects and Form
Visualisation, used with permission

top: The Sill's cafe windows beneath the cantilevered roof

above: Looking along the roof garden walk, in the direction of The Whin Sill

For non-geologists, or those unfamiliar with the beautiful Northumberland National Park, the name 'The Sill' must seem rather peculiar. In fact, The Sill is the term for an unusual, geological formation (on top of which Hadrian's Wall was built by the Romans). Sills are formed by magma moving upwards between sedimentary rock and then forcing its way between adjacent layers of sediment to form a horizontal 'table' of, in this case, dolerite stone (an igneous rock) and since this new rock is typically harder than the original sedimentary rock then after many millions of years of erosion the 'table' of igneous rock can end up being higher than the original stone, as is the case in The Whin Sill complex. Such a natural defensive structure would have been extremely useful to the Romans trying to defend the outer reaches of their empire, and in many respects Hadrian's Wall can be seen as a minor embellishment of an already formidable, natural 'wall' (as well as being useful for 'filling in' for those stretches where The Sill is less prominent). In terms of a setting, the visitor centre needs to take into account the needs of a World Heritage Site (the Hadrian's Wall World Heritage Site), a number of Scheduled Ancient Monuments (Hadrian's Wall is just one in this region) and a Site of Special Scientific Interest (due to its geological importance).

There was a previous visitor centre on the site, but it was small and considered unfit for purpose. Another feature of the site was that there was also an existing Youth Hostel Association hostel, first established in 1934, and the plan for the new visitor centre includes a new YHA hostel. This makes The Sill the only visitor centre studied in this book that has a hostel attached to it. It also means that the architect had, effectively, two clients and two very different sets of visitors' needs to accommodate. As is common for many of the visitor centres in this book, a competition was held for the design. The original Jane Darbyshire and David Kendall Architects (JDDK) competition-winning solution differed from the current design: the competition-winning design took its inspiration from the crystalline structure of the local, dolerite stone, producing a scheme characterised by sharp 'edges' and angles. However, after winning the completion JDDK

The Sill showing a detail of the stonework

and the Northumberland National Park Authority embarked on an extensive public participatory exercise, which led to the design gradually evolving into its current form.

The new visitor centre is located on the site of the old, on the B6318 (also known as The Military Road) and is about 600m south of Hadrian's Wall and the edge of The Whin Sill. In terms of land and topology, the site for the visitor centre lies lower than the edge of The Sill and Hadrian's Wall, as it is set into the slope of the land as it rises to its highest point at The Sill/the Wall. The new building is therefore designed to maximise the slope of the land by using this to reduce the overall bulk and visibility of the visitor centre from the surrounding landscape. In particular, the hostel section of the building is located at the lowest part of the site, and this helps to reduce the visual effect of the additional, 'blocky' mass of the hostel rooms. As the building climbs the slope, the cafe and its green roof above are both situated at the highest point of the site and have been angled to provide optimal views towards Peel Crags (the name of a particular rocky outcrop of The Sill). From inside the cafe, the entire façade facing The Sill forms one large curtain wall, meaning that the views out into the landscape will be unparalleled (it will probably be the best 'cup-of-tea-with-a-view' in Northumberland). The roof also slopes up to its highest point, just above, and partially sailing over, this picture window. The roof garden has been designed specifically with the views to the landscape in mind and has been planted with local plants, to replicate the unique, natural grasslands of the surrounding landscape, so that the roof surface is also, in effect, a growing exhibition of Northumbrian flora. The roof garden/walkway is accessed from The Military Road (and the point and direction from which walkers would arrive from Hadrian's Wall or depart towards it). The roof garden starts at ground level, just above the main exhibition space of the building, which is partially submerged into the ground, and so the visitor can simply walk straight up and onto the roof without hindrance. The gently angled, green ramp follows the slope of the first-floor roof, leading the visitor ever higher, crossing over and above the main entrance until suddenly the roof garden doubles back on itself and the visitor finds themselves, once again, facing towards the Whin Sill. Gradually they ascend to the second-floor level, this time walking over the main cafe, until eventually they reach the final lookout viewpoint. This linear roof garden, with its careful (and locally sourced planting) is strangely reminiscent of Diller and Scofidio's High Line linear park in New York, but obviously on a much smaller, more 'compressed' (and certainly far less urban) scale.

Other examples of 'local' detailing include the way that the relation between materials and the landscape has been carefully considered. Larch cladding has been used in conjunction with gabions: galvanised cages filled with local dolerite/basalt stone. The majority of these gabion cages have been placed on the North of the building facing towards the Whin Sill (the word 'Whin' means dark, hard rocks and so it is fitting that these stones are used on this side of the building). On the southern façade, softer sandstone has been used, reflecting the sedentary rocks, which form the other half of the geological story of The Sill. This sandstone comes from a local quarry in Haltwhistle.

Of all the buildings featured in this book, and visited as part of the research for it, this is the very last to be completed. Indeed, at the time of going to press, it was almost, but not quite, complete, however, by the time this book is published it will be open. Therefore, the first impressions of it are in its most raw state. Even at this stage, it is clear that this is a building that is not setting out to be iconic, but equally not one that seeks to disappear into the landscape (although once the gabion-stones start to acquire a smattering of moss, and the colour of the timber cladding softens to a neutral grey, the building will start to blend far more with the landscape than it does as present, being so implacably new). This clearly is a building that had strived to achieve the third way, to be synergistic, to take those aspects of the Northumberland National Park that make it such a unique place (the geology, the flora, the topology of the land) and design a building that not only reflects aspects of its 'exceptional setting' but help bring them to the foreground, to help focus the visitors' attention on them.

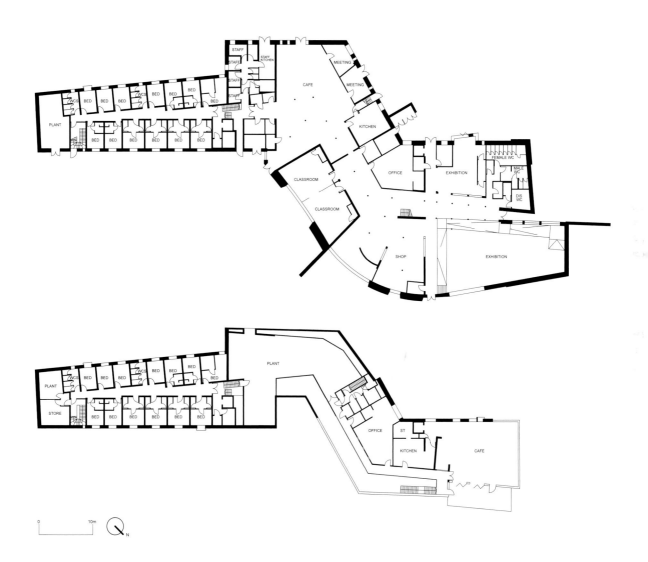

Plans of The Sill

Titan Crane

KEY FACTS

FULL NAME

Titan Clydebank: Education and Visitor Centre

ARCHITECTS

Collective Architecture Ltd

COMPLETION DATE

2011

COST

£121,000

COST/m²

£1,891

NEAREST POSTCODE

G81 1SE

SELECTED AWARDS

Institute of Mechanical Engineers, Engineering Heritage Award 2012

Civic Trust Awards × 2 2009

Chicago Athenaeum Award for Architecture 2008

The Titan Crane and visitor centre showing
the differences in scale between them

above: Interior of the Titan Crane visitor centre

top: Titan Crane reflected in the windows of
the visitor centre

above: Titan Crane visitor centre framed by
the base structure of the crane

The Titan Crane visitor centre is unique in many respects, and as such it is a delight to be able to include it in this book. First, it is the only visitor centre in the book that exists to celebrate and facilitate visiting a piece of industrial heritage and second, it is also particularly modest in terms of cost and scale. Given that some of the visitor centres featured in this book have had budgets of millions of pounds, it is good to know that great architectural design can come in all shapes and sizes. The Titan Crane visitor centre exists to support the visitors, approximately 3,000, who come during its opening season of May to October. But why should a crane, of all things, attract even 3,000 visitors a year? The Titan Crane was built in 1907 for the shipbuilders John Brown & Co Ltd and is located on the banks of the Clyde; specifically, the Crane is located on a dock (the Second Ward Dock) in what used to be the centre of Glasgow's shipbuilding district. In its heyday, the crane would have been located in the midst of a hive of industrial activity, surrounded by a forest of other cranes, the many buildings of the Clydebank Engineering & Shipbuilding Works and thousands upon thousands of workers. The crane is massive in scale: it is 150ft high (46m) and was the world's first electrically powered cantilever crane. When first constructed, it could lift 150 tons and was then subsequently upgraded in 1937 to lift 200 tons. Being part of the Clyde's shipbuilding industry it has been associated with the building of many famous ships including the Lusitania, the Queen Mary and the QE2. However, since the shipbuilding industry went into decline, all the other cranes and industrial buildings on the Clyde have been demolished, so that now, instead of being a massive structure in a sea of neighbouring cranes and buildings, the Titan Crane stands alone, as the most prominent and recognisable object on the Clydebank skyline.

The uniqueness of this structure was recognised by it being awarded an 'A' listed building status in 1988, which is the highest listed building status in Scotland. Today, the waterfront is partway through the process of being regenerated; the Titan Crane is therefore symbolic not only of Glasgow's rich and proud industrial heritage, but also symbolic of the ongoing regeneration of this area.

Collective Architecture (the architects) originally won a competition to develop a lighting strategy for the visually iconic crane, but it became evident that such a historically important structure merited more than some new lighting and so the plan to develop it as a visitor attraction began. Although the visitor centre can be considered to consist of the newly-built, free-standing cabin hunkering down at the foot of the crane (and which was originally intended to be integral to, rather than set apart from, the structure), the new lift that takes visitors to the top and the additional exhibitions located in the wheelhouse at the top of the crane can also be considered to be extensions of the visitor centre. In order to restore the crane, the entire structure needed to be shot-blasted back to raw steel before repainting. The new stair and lift were carefully inserted into the original steel frame of the structure (originally the lift was intended to be a small 'exhibition space' that simply happened to move vertically up and down). The lift shaft was clad in aluminium cladding and provided with windows so that as the visitors ascend to the top of the structure, fleeting glimpses of the structure can be seen on the way up (and down again). The top of the crane, which was once entirely open to the ground, has been floored with mesh panels and balustraded, meaning the visitors can walk around enjoying the views from above, before entering the former wheelhouse where further exhibitions and the lifting equipment can be viewed.

The crane and its visitor centre are located at the end of a U-shaped dock (the 'fitting out basin' of the former shipyard) about 200 metres long. The first proper glimpse of it (given that it is visible on the skyline for a long distance around it) is from the opposite side of the dock, over a distance of about 150 metres across the water, at the mouth of the dock. The visitor then has the strange (at least for architecture) experience of walking along the side of the dock, moving away from the crane and the building, being able to turn and glance back at it, with views of it against the bank of the Clyde, before turning the corner of the dock and re-approaching it head-on. And so from the moment of arrival at the entrance, it is a further half-kilometre round trip until actually reaching it, with the views of the crane and the building shifting constantly, as their relation to it changes.

In 'Whence and Whither', Philip Johnson talks about the importance of the 'processional element' in architecture. Johnson reminds his reader that 'whence' means 'where have you come from?' and 'whither' means 'where are you going?' The pro-cessional, for Johnson, is about the combination of understanding where you have come from while simultaneously looking forward to, and anticipating (both literally and figuratively) arriving. The circu-lar route to the Titan Crane gives not only ample time to view the crane from different angles, but in Johnson's true sense of the processional, gives time to appreciate the 'whence' and the 'whither'. The setting is one of flux; this is a landscape that is undergoing an almost unimaginable transfor-mation as the entire waterfront becomes regen-erated (for which the crane is, simultaneously, catalyst, bellwether and symbol). On one side of the dock the buildings of Clydebank College repre-sent the new, while on the other, on the former,

as-yet-to-be-regenerated former shipyards take on the appearance of the old: an alien, blasted planet. Here we have the first of our contrasts, for this is a building (or pair of buildings – pair of 'structures') of contrasts. The shiny new is juxtaposed against the desolate 'land-in-waiting': the future contrasted with the past. The crane and its visitor centre form another contrasting pair, this time a 'David and Goliath' pairing, the superlatively tall compared to the squat, the sea-spray blue of the crane (its traditional colour re-created) complemented by its opposite on the colour-wheel, the red-oxide of the visitor centre, the light and delicate lattice-work of the crane against the solid mass of the building, the 'whence' and the 'whither'. And yet, together they work compositionally, with the angled window of the visitor centre building (a humble shed or cabin really) appearing to look up at its antecedent as if in supplication. So, to end on the 'whence and the whither', the sense of the processional approach, the looking forward while looking back encapsulates the Titan Crane, is both a reminder of the proud past of the shipbuilding on the Clyde while looking forward to a future of which they are on the cusp.

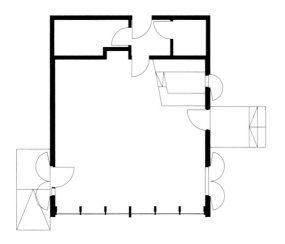

0   10m

N

Plan of Titan Crane

Welney Wetland Centre

KEY FACTS

FULL NAME
Welney Wetland Centre
ARCHITECTS
Allies and Morrison
COMPLETION DATE
2006
COST
Unavailable
COST/m²
Unavailable
NEAREST POSTCODE
PE14 9TN
SELECTED AWARDS
Civic Trust Awards Biodiversity Sensitivity Award 2007
RICS Awards RICS East Sustainability Award 2007
Green Apple Award for the Built Environment and Architectural Heritage 2007

Gable façade of Welney Wetland Centre

top: Pedestrian bridge over the New Bedford
River, looking from the Welney Wetland
Centre towards the wetlands

above: Long façade of Welney Wetland
Centre showing the double-height window
at the reception area

Welney Wetland Centre was built for The Wildfowl and Wetlands Trust in 2006 and is located nine miles north of Ely in an area of the country known as The Fens (a flat, low-lying region in the east of England, famous for its system of drainage channels and man-made dykes). The story behind the procurement of the building is an interesting one, as the original competition was to build not a visitor centre, but a bridge. In this case, a pedestrian bridge over the New Bedford River (also known as the Hundred Foot Drain), to allow visitors to cross over to the Welney Wetlands located in a flood plain situated between the New and the Old Bedford River (an internationally important area for wintering and breeding wildfowl and wading birds). Allies and Morrison's solution for a bridge for birdwatchers evolved into a visitor centre.

Formally, it is impossible to say whether this is a visitor centre with a bridge attached to it, or a bridge with a visitor centre attached to it. What is clear is that both halves, the bridge and the visitor centre, have equal prominence in the scheme and that the key to the successful resolution of the two parts is how they are integrated together into a single solution. As might be expected, the new bridge crosses the New Bedford River at an angle perpendicular to the river, and does so in a gentle curved arc. The visitor centre building is aligned parallel to the river, at right angles to the bridge. The formal diagram is a reversed L-shape, with the bridge as the stem of the 'L' and the visitor centre its leg. Because of the functional necessity for the bridge to pass over the South Level Barrier Bank (a flood-defensive dyke) the bridge meets the visitor centre at roof height rather than ground level (and visitors descend to ground level inside the building). Rather than the bridge simply disappearing into the building, the point at which the bridge meets the building is indicated, and celebrated, by removing a 'slice' from the building. The bridge simply 'touches' the building at this slot and so the visitor transitions from being on the bridge to being on a terrace (one of two terraces, an upper and a lower one) formed by the removal of part of the roof. The visitor centre building is a plain and simple extruded shape that forms an open gable roof but with unusual, rounded eaves. A second

'slot' balances the large 'slot', removed from the building; this time a large, double-height window facing the entrance area. If looking at the southeast façade, the building has a rotational symmetry, with this large window occupying the position of the terrace opening (if rotated through 180°).

The predominant material of the building is larch cladding; the same cladding for the walls is also used for the roof (and for the curved eaves) and so the overall effect is that the building has been carefully draped in a smooth and seamless skin of larch. Since the building was completed, the larch cladding has weathered to a mid-grey, but when the evening sun is low in the sky, the building glows a warm, golden colour.

On arrival, the first signs that you have reached your destination are the beautifully arched bridge over the river and the gable end of the visitor centre building, visible from the road. Entering the building on foot, from the car park, necessitates crossing over a smaller pedestrian bridge over a pond, although there is nothing architecturally significant about this bridge, it acts as a precursor to the main visitor activity, that of crossing the bridge (without which the birds cannot be seen). The building is entered from the northwest façade, which contains minimal openings and windows, and so the double-door main entrance, set into a glazed surround, is clearly indicative of its function. Once through the entrance space, the visitor is initially presented with views to the expanse of the landscape beyond. The reception desk is, unusually, on the first floor and once there, the generosity of the upper-floor spaces is immediately apparent. The floor to ceiling height is unusually tall, with a series of lights set into the apex of the roof (which is technically flat above the corridor). Large, full-height picture windows are placed along the walls of the cafe and look across the fens (and away from the river, which is not visible from the visitor centre due to the dyke). The slot in the building, which accommodates the start/end point of the bridge at roof-height, also forms a cafe-terrace at first-floor level. This terrace also features a large opening in the gable-end of the building, providing additional views along the dyke. The combination of formal simplicity and spatial

Welney Wetland Centre showing the two terraces set within the envelope of the building

complexity (with parts of the form removed to make external spaces) is particularly pleasing and is one of the compositional elements of this building that elevates it beyond being a mere reproduction of a rural barn (the other aspect of this building that ensures it cannot be 'read' as a vernacular building is the care taken in the detailing of the exterior: the seamless skin of timber cladding would never be found in a functional, rural building). It should also be noted that the architects managed to incorporate many sustainable features into the final building: ground source heat pumps; recycled paper insulation; a grey-water system; reed-bed water filtration; and sustainable timber. All of these formal, spatial, material and sustainable considerations serve to make this building one that clearly connects to its context in a sensitive and responsive manner.

In 2004, at the Architects' Journal/Bovis Awards dinner, Graham Morrison gave a talk entitled, 'The Trouble with Icons', where he said, 'Perhaps we should ask some simple questions before handing out more money and plaudits to "visionary" designers. What is the value of turning functional buildings into iconic ones? Are we simply trying too hard? Is a building's purpose compromised by its style? And what contribution does the icon make to its surroundings?' This is a particularly interesting speech in the context of this book, of visitor centres in general and in the context of the Welney visitor centre specifically. If you recall in Chapter 2, it was suggested that there were three approaches to designing buildings for 'exceptional settings', which is where most visitor centres are located. These were to design an iconic building (an approach that Graham Morrison questioned above), an invisible building or a synergistic building. In order to determine where the Welney visitor centre lies, let us turn Morrison's questions into reverse heuristics: i) functional buildings should not be iconic; ii) should not try too hard; iii) style should not compromise purpose; and iv) the building's contribution to its surroundings are an important consideration. I would suggest that the Welney does all of these things while at the same time, not falling into the trap of attempting to be too self-effacing (the hallmark of the 'invisible building'). In this case, it can be suggested that the Welney visitor centre comes very close to being a truly synergistic building.

Plans of Welney Wetland Centre

Whitby Abbey

FULL NAME

Whitby Abbey Visitor Centre

ARCHITECTS

Stanton Williams

COMPLETION DATE

2001

COST

£2,850,000

COST/m²

£5,700

NEAREST POSTCODE

YO22 4HG

SELECTED AWARDS

Europa Nostra Award 2003

RIBA Award 2003

Civic Trust Award 2003

RIBA White Rose Award 2002

RICS Award 2002

Religious
Archaeology
Ruin
Reuse

**Whitby Abbey, showing ruined, rear elevation
of the Banqueting Hall and rebuilt wall**

As part of Henry VIII's Dissolution of the Monasteries, Whitby Abbey was dissolved in 1539 and in 1555 the ruins, buildings and lands came into the ownership of the Cholmley family after being held on lease by them since the Reformation. From 1541 onwards the family started work on building a new house, which incorporated part of the former Abbot's House from the Abbey. The family also added a Jacobean hall (built 1672–83) now known as The Banqueting Hall (the site of the new visitor centre) and the Cholmley family lived here until the late 1700s. In 1775 the Banqueting Hall was destroyed in a great wind and never rebuilt. The empty windows of the banqueting house were subsequently filled in (presumably in order to stabilise the walls), and without any roof, the 'building' was simply three intact walls (the northern, front façade being one of the these) and an increasingly ruined fourth wall, the southern elevation. It remained in this state for over 200 years, and more recently was maintained as a 'controlled ruin' but never restored or reused. In 1997, English Heritage, Scarborough District Council and the Strickland-Constable estate began rationalising the entire abbey site and the new visitor centre, housed in the ruined Banqueting Hall, formed part of this scheme.

The problem of how to use a ruined shell for a new visitor centre is a particularly interesting one, and a range of options would have been available to the architects. They chose to leave the ruined walls of the Banqueting Hall untouched and instead to place a new steel-framed building inside the old ruins. The new, steel box-inside-a-box supports a new roof and only lightly touches upon the old structure. One of most challenging design questions must have been what to do with the windows of the imposing northern façade. For decades, these had been filled in, giving the building a haunting, blank look. Should they remain blocked up? Should they be replaced with wooden sash windows as would have been there originally? In fact, Stanton Williams decided to replace them with new, simply detailed, glazed windows with no mullions. Although seemingly incongruous to some visitors, it does however, echo the blankness and vacuity of the previous filled-in windows.

The experience of arriving at Whitby Abbey visitor centre is perhaps one of the most dramatic of those featured, as it is located high above the town on a natural headland looking out towards the sea. Although new car parks were part of the wider scheme for rationalising the Abbey estate, this is probably one of the few visitor centres at which most people arrive on foot, walking up The Church Stairs, a flight of 199 stone steps leading to the parish church. Probably a little breathless from the climb, the visitor emerges into a rather windswept, open space, from which the ruins of the abbey are clearly visible, as is a small information and ticketing office for English Heritage, but most of all what captures their attention will undoubtedly be the fine, old garden walls of the former Cholmley House. Set within these walls are a pair of late-seventeenth-century gatepiers that mark the main entrance to the original house. Passing through these gates, the visitor is immediately placed on a formal, symmetrical axis oriented towards the re-purposed, re-imagined and re-inhabited visitor centre. A stone path, with lawns on either side, leads them further towards the house, until reaching a cobbled forecourt, which was uncovered and restored as part of the works. In the centre of the forecourt sits a reconstruction of a seventeenth-century bronze statue, the 'Whitby Gladiator', based on the classical 'Borghese Gladiator' statue. Skirting around the forecourt, they finally arrive at the main entrance set in the centre of the north façade of The Banqueting Hall, in what would have been its main entrance.

Inside, the sense of being inside a new building, inside a ruin (i.e. a box in box) is not evident, which is a credit to the way in which the old and the new fit seamlessly together. The first observation is likely to be one of warmth, given by the deep honey colour of the English oak as set against the reds of the exposed brickwork. The steel frame is evident throughout, but is neither concealed, nor draws undue attention to it: it is simply there. The ruinous nature of the enclosing building is most evident at the rear of the building. This is revealed to the visitor if they move behind the welcome desk, with the intention of climbing the stairs to the second floor. It is this façade whose central section had

Main façade of Whitby Abbey visitor centre (the Banqueting Hall), showing a reflection of the 'Whitby Gladiator' in the windows

above: Whitby Abbey visitor centre from the bridge connecting the first floor of the Banqueting Hall to the abbey grounds

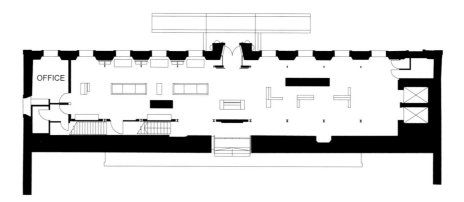

Ground Floor

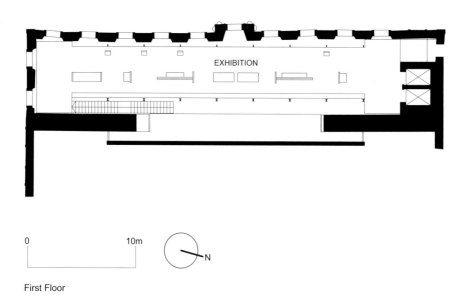

First Floor

Plans of Whitby Abbey

been all but destroyed, with the two outer sections partially intact. The treatment of this façade was to 'flip' the steel frame from being 'inside' the existing walls to 'outside' them, bringing the ruinous walls into the interior of the space. The external steel frame, at this point, is fitted with a glazed screen and louvres, since it is the south-facing façade and direct sunlight could otherwise be problematic. The visual contrast between the jagged edges of the ruined walls, thrown into sharp relief against the smooth surfaces and even rhythms of the new external wall, serves to heighten the visitor's awareness of the materiality of the older building; the blend of the old and new has been handled very deftly. A single flight of stairs is located in a slot formed between the ruined southern façade and the line of structural steel columns. This slot runs the full length of the building and is the clearest intent of the desire to separate fully the new from the old. Arriving at the second floor, into a single open space, views of the Abbey in the far distance can be seen through the re-opened windows. These Abbey-scenes were clearly the views enjoyed by the Cholmley family when the house was first built, views not seen for centuries and it is a rare pleasure to see them reinstated.

The access to the Abbey is via the first floor of the visitor centre, where a glass bridge has been constructed, linking this upper floor level to the Abbey grounds. (Access is also available via two lifts, the abbey grounds having been made more accessible since the completion of the visitor centre). Many visitor centres seem to feature bridges, often for practical reasons, and here it is about bridging differences in ground levels, while symbolically marking the entrance to the Abbey ruins. Once into the Abbey grounds, just as views to the Abbey were revealed from the visitor centre, so the visitor is able to look back and appreciate the restored façade of Cholmley House from the higher elevation of the Abbey ruins; the relationship between the buildings and ruins is particularly strong. For a site that is predominately about the ruined and the picturesque, the visitor centre is one of the best examples of how to blend old and new without either becoming more dominant or detracting from the other: it reflects a dialogue between the two parts.

Interior, Whitby Abbey visitor centre showing juxtaposition of the old and the new

Wycoller Aisled Barn

KEY FACTS

FULL NAME
Wycoller Aisled Barn

ARCHITECTS
Hakes Associates

COMPLETION DATE
2002

COST
£100,000

COST/m²
Unavailable

NEAREST POSTCODE
BB8 8SY

SELECTED AWARDS
RIBA Award 2002
Shortlisted for the Stephen Lawrence Award

History
Landscape
Reuse
Writer

View along the L-shaped platform inside
Wycoller Aisled Barn with the Corten display
wall to the right

top: Ruins of Wycoller Hall ('Ferndean Manor')
seen through the glass wall of Wycoller Aisled
Barn's visitor 'pod'

above: Display wall and illuminated display
boxes, Wycoller Aisled Barn

Wycoller Aisled Barn is a fascinating example of a visitor centre since it is one of the few visitor centres in this book that demonstrates exquisitely the reuse of a much older building, built for an entirely different function (in this case it was an agricultural barn), and transformed into a visitor centre. The other key example, to which it can be usefully compared is Whitby Abbey visitor centre, however, compared to Whitby Abbey (which reused a grand yet ruinous Banqueting Hall) this visitor centre is noteworthy for being particularly modest in cost and scale, to the extent that it potentially defies the definition of visitor centre. To dispel any doubts as to whether this really is a visitor centre or not, then the definition of a visitor centre needs to be re-examined briefly. First and foremost is the importance of 'place' to the visitor centre (see Chapter 1). It is clear that a visitor centre can only be located in its current setting and that the relationship between the visitor centre and its surrounding landscape and context is critical to its function. By this definition, and the emphasis on place, there is no doubt that the Aisled Barn at Wycoller is a visitor centre. The barn is an exemplar of a regional, vernacular, agricultural building and its immediate context oozes 'place-ness'. Another criterion was that the presence of visitors typically (although not always) predates the construction of the visitor centre; this was also true in the case of Wycoller Hall and village. Finally, the visitor centre should not be about 'acquiring knowledge' (as in a museum), and that the main exhibit (in this case the 'attraction' is the village of Wycoller and its adjacent moors) dominates the visiting experience. On the basis of all of these, it can be stated that, despite its bijou size, Wycoller Aisled Barn is a visitor centre.

Wycoller is a small, remote and scenic village to the east of the county of Lancashire, on the border with the former West Riding of Yorkshire and, most importantly, just over six and a half miles, across the moors, from the Parsonage in Haworth, home of the Brontës. The Brontë connection is particularly important to Wycoller, as immediately next to the Aisled Barn are situated the highly picturesque ruins of Wycoller Hall (at one stage the Aisled Barn was used as a coach house for the Hall), thought to

be the inspiration for Ferndean Manor to which Mr Rochester retreats after the fire at Thornfield (*Jane Eyre*). This connection with the Brontës is celebrated in the material fabric of the visitor centre via an etched, glazed panel, placed over one of the barn's openings, which bears a quotation from Charlotte Brontë's novel, *Shirley*, in which she describes a stream – its 'broken, unquiet course, struggling with many stones, chafing against rugged banks, fretting with gnarled tree-roots, foaming, gurgling, battling as it went ...'. This text could certainly have been describing the Wycoller Beck as it flows past the Aisled Barn. As is evident in its name, the barn is a double-aisled barn, with five bays, built around 1630 and aligned approximately north–south. Given that it was built on the site of an earlier cruck (or crook-framed) barn, then it is possible that some of the timbers from the earlier barn may have been reused in the later, and hence some timbers present in the present barn may date from 1533.

The new visitor centre is the result of a number of sensitive insertions into the historic barn, broadly consisting of three items: a raised platform; a curved glass 'pod'; and a low, thick, illuminated display 'wall' punctured with exhibits. The primary aim of the architects was to minimise the impact on the Grade II-listed interior of the barn and therefore everything was designed not to be fixed into the existing material structure but rather to be self-supporting and hence ultimately removable if necessary. The unifying element of the barn's new 'insertions' is the raised platform, which is essentially L-shaped and fills one entire bay (of the five) at the south end of the barn (forming the 'foot' of the L). This platform also runs the entire length of the barn and has been slotted in between the outer wall and the main aisle or arcade posts of the post-and-beam structure. This new wooden platform has been made of grooved cumaru (or Brazilian teak) decking, and hence not un-reminiscent of garden decking; it is supported by an array of stainless steel legs, each on its own base and each individually adjustable to accommodate the considerable unevenness in the original cobbled, stone floor. The raised platform abuts the irregular stones of the barn's walls, but is, importantly, not supported by them. A ramp

Interior, Wycoller Aisled Barn showing a detail
of the barn's stylobates and the edge of the
Corten display wall

leads from the original wooden floor up to the main
'foot' of the L-shape, at the south end of the barn.
As mentioned above, the L-shaped platform acts as
the unifying structure that connects the glass 'pod'
at the southwest corner of the barn with the long
display wall running down the eastern side of the
barn, located between the stone wall and the line of
arcade posts supported by the high stone stylobates
(foundation base stones).

The display wall is approximately head-height
and is formed of Corten sheets. Each end of the
Cor-Ten display wall is lined with translucent white
glass housing a concealed light source; these illuminated panels at either end serve to punctuate the
wall, marking its endpoints. These end-panels are
also echoed by a series of display boxes, randomly
inserted along the length of the wall, since the same
white glass panels are set into the reveals of these
'holes'. The third new addition to the barn is the
glass pod. The design of the pod makes it appear as
if part of the raised platform has been simply lifted
and curved over itself in order to provide protection
for the visitor (the glass sides have been inserted
with minimal detailing so as to not to detract from
this impression). A sign in the barn, describing the
glass 'pod', explains, 'We have provided room for
... the lone walker ... who will find a warm wall for
comfort on a cold winter's day'.

Arriving at the Aisled Barn is a memorable
experience, due to the picturesque setting beside
the babbling Wycoller Beck. The visitor enters the
barn and their first impression, coming in from the
bright outside is one of gloom: the atmosphere feels
thick with age. But the careful lighting immediately
draws the attention: it is not so harsh that it disrupts
the cool, dark atmosphere of the barn, but is sufficient light that forms and textures are accentuated.
The visitor's eye is drawn to the curves of the glass
pod and the illuminated white glass reveals at the
ends of the display wall. The texture of the ancient
timbers is matched by the textures and rich colours
of the Corten steel, the grooved cumaru decking and
the smooth glass. Being in this space, the visitor
understands and appreciates that these interventions are subtle and respectful.

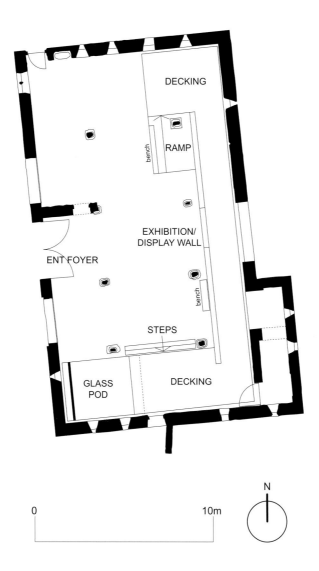

DECKING

RAMP

bench

EXHIBITION/
DISPLAY WALL

bench

ENT FOYER

STEPS

GLASS
POD

DECKING

0   10m

N

Indicative plan of Wycoller Aisled Barn
Source: Based on a survey by David
Michelmore of Building Conservation
Services and redrawn by the author, showing
the approximate position of the new visitor
centre 'insertions'

Notes

Preface and Acknowledgements

1. *Take One Building: Interdisciplinary Research Perspectives of the Seattle Central Library*, edited by Ruth Conroy Dalton and Christoph Hölscher. Abingdon: Taylor and Francis, 2016.

2 Place, Landscape and the Visitor Centre

1. *The Ascent of Man* documentary series was first broadcast by the BBC in 1973. Reading this quote in the twenty-first century, please read 'man' to indicate 'humans', 'human beings', 'people', etc.

2. Personal correspondence with David Seamon, 7 November 2016.

3. In a paper on travel behaviour to National Trust properties in the South West of England, repeat visitors constituted 41 per cent, whereas first time visitors represented 59 per cent, of people sampled by Dickinson et al. (2004).

4. Novels about Stonehenge include: Bernard Cornwell, *Stonehenge* (1999); Cecelia Holland, *Pillar of the Sky* (1985); Eileen Kernaghan, *The Sarsen Witch* (1989); J.P. Reedman, *Stone Lord* (2012); J.P. Reedman, *Moon Lord* (2012); Lindsay Townsend, *Bronze Lightning* (2009); Hebe Weenolsen, *The Forbidden Mountain* (1983); Edward Rutherfurd, *Sarum: The Novel of England* (1987) to name but a few novels set near Stonehenge.

5. Approximately 16 films have used Stonehenge as a setting.

6. The 'density' of a place is simply the idea that some locations evoke such a strong sense of place (relative to others), and that this can be concentrated in a relatively small geographic location or site and so the 'density' of place is quite high.

7. At the end of the process you also receive a calculation of your internal consistency so you can check that you've been as (internally) consistent as you can be (below 10 per cent consistency is good). Ideally this is performed by several evaluators and the results combined.

3 The Visitor

1. Almost by definition, the 'explorer' could never expect to find a visitor centre waiting for them.

4 The Archetypal Visitor Centre

1. *Source:* VisitEngland Data.

2. *Source:* Private correspondence.

Bibliography

Agnew, J. (1987). *Place and Politics. The Geographical Mediation of State and Society*. Boston and London: Allen & Unwin

Argan, G.C. (1963). 'On the Typology of Architecture', in Nesbitt, K. (ed.) (1996), *Theorizing a New Agenda for Architecture: An Anthology of Architectural Theory 1965–1995*. New York: Princeton Architectural Press, pp. 242–6. Trans. by Joseph Rykwert and originally published in *Architectural Design*, no. 33. December 1963: 564–5

Bafna, S. (2001). 'Geometric Intuitions of Genotypes', in *Proceedings of 3rd International Space Syntax Symposium*, Atlanta 2001, 20.1–20.16 (p. 20.2)

Benedikt, M. (2001). 'Reality and authenticity in the experience economy', *Architectural Record*, 189 (11): 84–87

Bernstein, B. (1975). *Class, Codes and Control Vol. 3: Towards a Theory of Educational Transmissions*. London: Routledge and Kegan Paul

Casey, E.S. (1993). *Getting Back into Place: Toward a Renewed Understanding of the Place-World*. Bloomington: Indiana University Press

Cassirer, E. (1951). *The Philosophy of the Enlightenment*. Princeton, NJ: Princeton University Press

Coates, N. (2012). *Narrative Architecture*. Chichester: John Wiley & Sons

Cormack, B. (1998). *A History of Holidays, 1812–1990* (Vol. 4). Abingdon: Routledge/Thoemmes

Cresswell, T. (2004). *Place: A Short Introduction* (Short Introductions to Geography). Chichester: Wiley-Blackwell

Dalton, R. (2016). 'OMA's Conception of the Users of Seattle Central Library', in Dalton, R. and Hölscher, C. (eds) *Take One Building: Interdisciplinary Research Perspectives of the Seattle Public Library*. Abingdon: Routledge

Davis, M.H. (1983). 'Measuring individual differences in empathy: Evidence for a multidimensional approach', *Journal of Personality and Social Psychology*, 44(1): 113

Davis, M.H., Conklin, L., Smith, A. and Luce, C. (1996). 'Effect of perspective taking on the cognitive representation of persons: a merging of self and other', *Journal of Personality and Social Psychology*, 70(4): 713

Department for Transport (2014). National Travel Survey: 2014. Available at www.gov.uk/government/statistics/national-travel-survey-2014. Accessed 25 February 2017

Dickinson, J.E., Calver, S., Watters, K. and Wilkes, K. (2004). 'Journeys to heritage attractions in the UK: A case study of National Trust property visitors in the south west', *Journal of Transport Geography*, 12(2): 103–13

Dovey, K. (1985). 'The quest for authenticity and the replication of environmental meaning' in Seamon, D. and Mugerauer, R. (eds), *Dwelling, Place and Environment: Towards a Phenomenology of Person and World*. Dordrecht: Martinus Nijhoff Publishers, pp. 33–49

Fees Craig, F. (1996). 'Tourism and the Politics of Authenticity in a North Cotswold Town' in Selwyn, T. (ed.) *The Tourist Image: Myths and Myth Making in Tourism*. New York: John Wiley & Sons, pp. 121–47

Fussell, P. (1982). *Abroad: British Literary Traveling Between the Wars*. New York: Oxford University Press

Glancey, J. (2014). 'AJ100 #8: Jonathan Glancey on Allies and Morrison', *The Architects' Journal*. Available at: www.architectsjournal.co.uk/home/aj100-8-jonathan-glancey-on-allies-and-morrison/8662844.article. Accessed 2 February 2017

Henley, J. (2010). 'How the National Trust is finding its mojo', *The Guardian*, 10 February. Available at www.theguardian.com/culture/2010/feb/10/national-trust-opens-its-doors. Accessed 2 February 2017

Hillier, B., Hanson, J. and Graham, H. (1987). 'Ideas are in things: an application of the space syntax method to discovering house genotypes', *Environment and Planning B*: 14: 363–85

Hillier, B. (1996). *Space is the Machine: A Configurational Theory of Architecture*. Cambridge: Cambridge University Press

Hood, M.G. (1983). 'Staying away – Why people choose not to visit museums', *Museum News* 61(4): 50–57

Johnson, P. (1965). 'Whence and whither: the processional element in architecture', *Perspecta* (The Yale Architectural Journal), 9/10: 167–78

MacCannell, D. (1973). 'Staged Authenticity: Arrangements of Social Space in Tourist Settings', *The American Journal of Sociology*, 79(3): 589-603

Masberg, B.A. and Silverman, L.H. (1996). 'Visitor Experiences at Heritage Sites: A Phenomenological Approach', *Journal of Travel Research*, 34(4): 20–25

Niles, R. (2006). *Robert Niles' Journalism Help: Statistics Every Writer Should Know*. Available at RobertNiles.com. Accessed 19 February 2017, www.robertniles.com/stats/

Ousby, I. (2002). *The Englishman's England: Taste, Travel, and the Rise of Tourism*. London: Pimlico

Piaget, J. ([1932]1965). *The Moral Judgment of the Child*. New York: The Free Press

Psarra, S. (2009). *Architecture and Narrative: The Formation of Space and Cultural Meaning*. Abingdon: Routledge

Quatremère de Quincy, A-C. (1825). 'Type', in *Encyclopédie Méthodique*, Vol. 3 (Paris). Translated by Tony Vidler, *Oppositions* 8, Spring, 1977, p. 148

Rayport, J.F. and Leonard-Barton, D. (1997). 'Spark Innovation Through Empathic Design', *Harvard Business Review*, November–December: 107–19

Relph, E. (2008). *Place and Placelessness*. London: Pion (Original work published 1976)

Seamon, D. (1987). 'Phenomenology and Environment–Behavior Research' in Moore, G.T. and Zube, E. (eds), *Advances in Environment, Behavior, and Design*, Vol. 1. New York: Plenum Press, pp. 3–22

Seamon, D. (1992). 'A Diary Interpretation of Place: Artist Frederic Church's Olana', in Janelle, D.G. (ed.) *Geographical Snapshots of North America*. New York: Guilford Press, pp. 78–82

Smith, J. (1771). *Choir gaur; the grand orrery of the ancient Druids, commonly called Stonehenge, … astronomically explained, and mathematically proved to be a temple … three copper plates*. Andover: Gale ECCO (Eighteenth Century Collections Online)

Tenbrink, T., Hölscher, C., Tsigaridi, D. and Dalton, R.C. (2014). 'Cognition and Communication in Architectural Design' in Montello, D.R., Grossner, K. and Janelle, D.G. (eds) *Space in Mind: Concepts for Spatial Learning and Education*. Cambridge, MA: MIT Press

Thiel, P. (1997). *People, Paths, and Purposes: Notations for a Participatory Envirotecture*. Seattle: University of Washington Press

Thompson, D. (1991). 'An Architectural View of the Visitor-Museum Relationship' in Bitgood, S. Benefield, A. and Patterson, D. (eds) *Visitor Studies: Theory, Research, and Practice*, 3. Jacksonville: Center for Social Design, pp. 72–85

VisitEngland (2016). Visitor Attraction Trends in England 2015: Full Report. Available at www.visitbritain.org/sites/default/files/vb-corporate/Documents-Library/documents/England-documents/annual_visitor_attractions_trends_in_england_2015.pdf. Accessed 26 November 2016

Weber, R. (1995). *On the Aesthetics of Architecture: A Psychological Approach to the Structure and the Order of Perceived Architectural Space (Ethnoscapes)*. Aldershot: Avebury

Woodall, R. (1976). *Magnificent Derelicts: A Celebration of Older Buildings*. Vancouver: J.J. Douglas Ltd

Zumthor, P. (2006). *Atmospheres: Architectural Environments – Surroundings Objects*. Basel: Birkhäuser

Index

Page numbers in *italics* refer to captions.